Praise for *Secr*

"One of our numerous resolutions is to be more optimistic, so when we got a copy of this hysterical book, we knew we were on the right track."

—ROLLING STONE

"This volume could become the self-help of choice for people who don't read self-help. A quirky, unique primer, it provides more than 100 points of advice for achieving SuperOptimism, defined as "the mental discipline to reframe any situation into a favorable outcome." Morton and Whitten provide plenty of fresh perspective from way out in left field."

—PUBLISHER'S WEEKLY

"Incredibly smart and funny...Our favorite secret? Saving the truth for special occasions."

—THESMOKINGGUN.COM

"A host of fresh insights that manage to enlighten and entertain. My recommendation: a solid dose of SuperOptimism."

—HUFFINGTON POST

"Fact-based psychology meets punk rock sensibility. This book will help you survive the cultural pitfalls of the 21st Century."

—DAN KENNEDY
Author and Host of The Moth Storytelling Podcast

"Unlike virtually any other self-help book you will read."

—BLOGCRITICS

The SUPEROPTIMIST
Guide to Unconventional Living

Within these pages,
you shall find:

Calculated risks
Contrarian takes
Rational alternatives
Fresh perspectives
Supportive frameworks
Productivity boosters
Dream catalysts
Travel suggestions
Personality indicators
Classic nostrums
Mathematical constants
Spirit channels
Elvis quotes
Lawncare tips

And also:

Happy thoughts
Scientific formulas
Tolerance exercises
Natural wonders
Timeless parables
Breakfast suggestions

Also by Nathaniel Whitten & Walter Morton

Secrets of the SuperOptimist

By Nathaniel Whitten

The Do-It-Yourself Constitutional Amendment Kit

A Wise Man Taught Me How to Defy Gravity and Now I'll Teach You

The Book of Extremely Common Prayer

By Walter Morton

American Ghoul

The SUPEROPTIMIST
Guide to Unconventional Living

Alternative Strategies for Navigating the Present

Nathaniel Whitten and Walter Morton

New York San Francisco London Tokyo Forestville

Manufactured in the United States of America

Published by Vitally Important Books
www.vitallyimportant.com

1st Edition, August 2022
Limited Printing
Paperback ISBN: 978-0-9774807-8-4
eBook ISBN: 978-0-9774807-9-1

SuperOptimist!

www.superoptimist.com
SUPEROPTIMIST®

SuperOptimism is not to be confused with plain old ordinary optimism or other extropian principles, including the following: Utopianism, Intelligent Technology, Perpetual Progress, Self-Direction, Emotional Life Expansion, or Dynamic Tension.

Printed in the United States of America
20 19 18 17 16 15 14 13 12 11 10 9 8 7 6 5 4 3 2 1

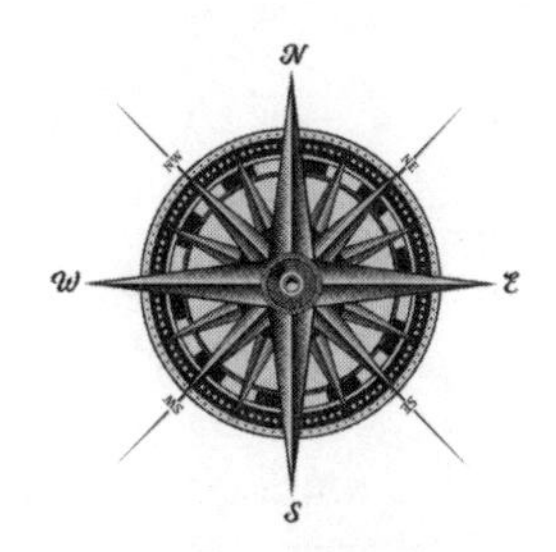

TABLE OF CONTENTS

THE SECRETS

ADDENDA

APPENDICES

PREFACE

In 2007, the Class 2 philosophy known as "SuperOptimism" entered the lexicon. As published in the book *Secrets of the SuperOptimist*, the first 116 wisdom transmissions became the foundation of a practice focused on discovering the positive in each and every situation one might face. By committing to a program of "active reframing," one could remain relaxed, secure, and engaged — even when lost, sequestered, unemployed, hospitalized, incarcerated, or losing big at blackjack.

The volume you now hold in your hands is the product of additional research in navigating the swirling eddies of human existence. Recent global events have led many to question the time they have left on earth, with particular emphasis on "What do I do now?" and "Something's got to give." In addition to honing an ultra-positive approach to the here and now, *The SuperOptimist Guide to Unconventional Living* instructs the reader on dynamic ways to sidestep social constructs that have become calcified in homo sapiens over centuries. By refusing to accept the systemetized version of reality, we are able to seek new adventure in ways both small, medium and extra large.

Place these arrows in your personal quiver and you'll find the established course of daily affairs will be no match for your ability to transcend the ordinary — with positivity, humor and spirit intact.

INTRODUCTION

When one person, for whatever reason, has a chance to lead an exceptional life, he has no right to keep it to himself.
-Jacques Cousteau

We celebrate the nonconformists in society, hailing them as brave risk-takers deserving of our respect. Their contrarian approach to a safe, secure existence is counter-intuitive; we marvel at their ability to plunge into the icy river of uncertainty without thinking twice (and sans wetsuit). We could live this way too — if only we didn't have the responsibilities, routines, and practical sides that hold us back.

Where have these responsibilities and routines come from? As the Industrial Age has given way to the Digital Revolution, estimates now place 89% of our brain function as habitual robotic reactions to circumstance, whether it's checking our phones, working at repetitive tasks, binge-watching television, or wearing shoes. For most of us, this psychosocial programming has followed us from childhood through adulthood and conditions all aspects of our thinking. We adhere to the patterns year in and year out, whether we are bored or engaged, content or disheartened. Only when we stop and ask ourselves the key question “why do I think the way I do?” can we begin to embrace more compelling options.

Examine how you've acquired your beliefs. Which authority figures told you what was right and wrong? What system was responsible for your education? Who were your friends? These and other factors determine whether you are guarded or gregarious, open-minded or dogmatic, and even extend to your understanding about what is “good” and “bad.” The questions then become, “Is any of it true? Is it possible to revise the narrative? Can I deactivate the autopilot and rekindle my fascination with the moment at hand?"

"Yes!" is the answer and now is the time. In the following pages, you’ll find countless ways to disengage from the commonplace and open your neural pathways to more expansive thinking. By adopting a program of “positive self-provocation,” an exceptional way of life will be yours.

Start by considering the word "abandon." At first blush, this would seem to be an experience to avoid. Yet in French, the word “abandon” also means “Freedom from constraint.” This book offers 105 experiments and activities to help you abandon the shackles of conformity. With practice, we're confident you'll find the sparks to ignite many inspiring, if unpredictable, new exploits. Bonne chance!

— The Authors

BEFORE YOU BEGIN

3. There is no predetermined order in which to carry out these experiments and activities. We find the element of surprise adds energy to the practice. Thus, we have placed the suggestions nonsequentially in order to mimic the randomness one finds in the universe.

1. While we encourage you to use this book as you see fit, scientific study has proven that SuperOptimism is best absorbed one wisdom transmission at a time.

2. Just as there is no doctor's prescription that suits every patient, nor a preacher's directive that stirs every soul, we give the reader full license to deploy the secrets they find most helpful, while putting the rest aside.

Venite incipere

SECRET #137

Set a different alarm.

Routines can be mind-numbing. So why start your day with one? Why not wake up at a different time on Monday than you do on Wednesday? It doesn't always have to be 7 a.m. Why not 5:00 tomorrow? And 7:30 the next? What about getting up at 4:00 a.m. and seeing what's going on outside? What about "no alarm day," where you don't ever leave your bed? Or "double alarm day," where you sleep for four hours at one stretch and then four hours at another?

These are merely suggestions. But the thrill in deviating from one's well-worn path is worth it, even if it's for fifteen minutes at a time. The shock to your system could knock loose a new idea — or a whole new way of life. Besides, you can always take a nap later.

SECRET #132

Behold the answer you're searching for.

Whether it's a cure for procrastination, a way to beat the stock market, or the one diet that will help you shed pounds without giving up coconut cream pie, there's no lack of people willing to offer you "the answer." Yet why don't the experts' directives live up to their hype? Because the true answer is *there is no answer.*

Each life is a curious amalgam of genetic markers, family skeletons, previous experiences, and standardized test scores. There is no one-size-fits-all answer in any category. Nor can anyone give you assurance that the path you are on will lead to your hoped-for destination.

"Abandon the search for reason" is the ancient Daoist healing practice to unshackle you from the desperate need to get things right. When the questions arise in your mind, like "Why me?" or "Where is God now?" or "Who put soy milk in my no-foam latte?," you can be freed of the burden of having to find the answer before your time on earth is up.

As for the bellicose authors, control-freak life coaches, and cardboard spiritualists with their proclamations of 30-day miracles, you can confidently answer their come-ons with the powerful understanding that they do not have "the answer" — for in fact, there isn't one.*

**However, if you find yourself in legal trouble, make sure you consult an experienced attorney.*

SECRET #134

Carry one of these at all times.

Lemons have suffered from an image problem for eons. Not only does the word “lemon” refer to a substandard product — most typically a used car — but it’s also used to mean “disappointing result” or “something unwanted."

Perhaps this is due to their stinging acidity and tough skins (although both are considered positive traits in news columnists and football coaches). But as any SuperOptimist can tell you, it pays to seek the truth for yourself.

Lemons are healthy fruits, rich in vitamin C and other nutrients, used in a myriad of wonderful products, from lemonade to lemon meringue pie. Even better, lemons are a natural way to gain control over spiritual forces in the universe. They’ve been used for years by Feng Shui practitioners and Buddhist monks to keep negative energies at bay and enhance both health and mood. By placing a lemon in your pocket and taking it with you as you travel, you can protect yourself from the bad vibes you may encounter while you’re on the go.*

On the home front, you can stop discord from entering and spreading through your domicile by cutting a lemon into four and spreading salt on each slice. Then place the slices at the entrance to your house and the lemon will absorb the creepiness from anyone who comes to your door.

What's more, sleeping next to a cut-up lemon on your nightstand will add to your positive energy, as lemons have been used as a powerful aromatherapy oil for ages. Increased concentration, decreased stress levels and smoother respiratory activity are just some of the benefits the night-time lemon will have on your health. Pleasant dreams.

**A lemon can dry up rapidly depending on how much negative energy you encounter. Make sure you replace your lemon with a fresh one, especially if you visit Washington, DC.*

SECRET #191

Praise those who ignore your instructions.

July 3rd is the anniversary of Franz Kafka's birth. Yet while we are indebted to this author for his unique vision, we prefer to roll out the sheet cake for his friend Max Brod. If not for dear Max, we'd have no idea who Franz Kafka even was.

In failing health and having received little acknowledgment for his storytelling efforts, Kafka entrusted his lifelong pal to destroy all his unpublished work upon his death. But when Franz finally met his maker, Brod ignored his deceased friend's wishes. Instead of torching Kafka's manuscripts, he had them published instead.

Without Brod making that fateful decision, Kafka might have remained an anonymous insurance man who wrote fiction on the side. And we would not have *The Trial*, *The Castle* or *Amerika* to read, ponder and cherish. So each July 3rd, we give thanks for Max Brod — and the reminder that it's occasionally beneficial to listen to voices other than our own.

SECRET #144

The most important day of your life.

It's a scientific fact that this is the only __________ *(place today's date here)* you will ever experience. How can you ensure that it's spectacular? Start by taking a deep breath. Ahhh. Feel the rush of oxygen clearing out those cobwebs. Now go stand outside for a few minutes. Sun, rain, snow... no matter what the weather, the planet is here to offer you a world of possibility. It makes sense to embrace it. Finally, shout at the top of your lungs: "Today is going to be the best day ever!" By proclaiming your intention to make this one a winner, you are 130% more likely to experience it that way. *

These simple actions will set you on a course for a super-duper morning. And if you need a refresher, double down after lunch.

**At the very least, buy a lottery ticket. This will seal the deal.*

SECRET #118

Burn the bridge. Enjoy the warmth.

The expression "burn one's bridge" comes from the very act of burning down a wooden crossing after marching over it during a military campaign, leaving no choice but to continue moving forward while making it more difficult for your enemies to follow. When there's no turning back, you have only your goal to go.

Right or wrong, sane or mad, to set out on a course of action and eliminate any route of escape reduces the chance of compromise. Think of Ahab and his pursuit of the great white whale. He could have cut bait, steered the boat back to harbor, propped up his feet and puffed on a fat cigar. Instead, nothing would deter him from that final face-off with the great Moby D. Of course, things didn't turn out pleasantly for the captain. But there's no arguing that it made for a more striking obituary.

And herein lies the point. It's the story you wind up with that's important. Who wants to die sitting in an easy chair trying to digest another big meal? Lashed to a monstrous mammal with your own rope? Now that's the way to go!

Achieving a goal requires total commitment, even at the risk of leaving behind a job, a relationship or a soft, comfortable couch that beckons to you when the pursuit becomes difficult in the extreme. Here's to pushing off from shore and pursuing your whale to the very end.

The international symbol for "no turning back." Place it in your wallet as a reminder.

SECRET #158

Staring can be good for your health.

A recent study found that a single hour in an art museum improved a person's attitude and demeanor, though you needn't battle the crowds at MOMA to have an epiphany. Sitting in the kitchen staring at a bowl of peaches can be just as impactful.

Set a timer for five minutes. Now look directly at the fruit without averting your gaze and observe the peach with all your senses. How would you describe it? Smooth? Fuzzy? Small? How many colors do you see? You'll find that the act of quiet observation helps promote the feeling of escape.

While staring at the peaches, ask yourself: How did they arrive in that bowl? How did the bowl arrive on the table? Who grew the peaches? Who picked them? Who packed them? Who shipped them? Consider the connectivity of the universe, the peaches and you. The longer you stare at the peaches, the more likely you are to experience "the Troxler effect," a phenomenon first identified by Ignaz Troxler in 1804. When certain stimuli have been consistently hitting your senses for a while, mild hallucinations may occur as you disassociate and depart from reality. The shift away from concrete details and towards abstract ideas can lead to amazing thoughts. What comes to mind? Try it with a bowl of cereal tomorrow.

SECRET #139

All dreams are good. Especially the bad ones.

Seducing the fairest of them all. Waving from an open convertible along the Canyon of Heroes. Discovering a gold-filled treasure chest. Sure, these are great fantasies and worthy of major REM activity. But think about it: emerging from a pleasant dream into the harsh light of reality is a brutal way to wake up.

It's actually more comforting to come to after experiencing a twisted nightmare. What a relief to open your eyes and realize a flock of giant vultures aren't feasting on your intestines. Once you acknowledge that you haven't actually lost a limb to a tiger shark or been fondled by your father, you can be even more grateful for the day ahead.

So celebrate all dreams, especially the god-awful ones. They can give you a new lease on life. Like that one where you're standing naked in front of your grade school classmates, forgetting the words to a Carl Sandburg poem.

Bonus tip: Researchers at Goethe University advise us to avoid repressing undesired thoughts at bedtime. This way, they're less likely to find their way into our dreams that night.

SECRET #161

The more time on your hands, the better.

"I'm crazy busy" is now a frequent refrain of the upper classes. Despite the negative connotations of being crazy — i.e. "mentally unhinged" — it is used as a symbol of status, the implication being that one's life is full to overflowing between work, family and recreation. Many believe that without an overloaded schedule, they will veer into sinfulness and sloth if they go slack for any length of time.

On the other hand, not working so much may be the enlightened path forward. Indian Yogis have known the power of being idle for centuries, sitting in meditation to gain power, aura, and knowledge from the state of idleness. Doing absolutely nothing can really be something, as Shiva and his followers can attest.

So rather than idleness being the devil's workshop, reversing our mad dash towards full productivity may be the true way to keep Satan from claiming our souls.

SECRET #117

Fight fatigue the Sufi way.

Wishing you could beat the exhaustion that arrives every afternoon at 3 p.m.? Take your cue from a dervish and become your own "spin doctor."

By focusing on the heavens and turning around and around in a tight circle, you can reach "Kemal" — the source of all perfection. How does this happen? For one thing, you get a vigorous workout that raises your endorphins. For another, your mind can't focus on lethargy when it's working overtime trying to keep you upright.

Many dervishes start their practice with a cup of strong Turkish coffee, to which we heartily subscribe. And if you're looking for an appropriate song to accompany your footwork, try "Peşrev in maqām acem." You'll be spinning like an Istanbulite in no time.

REVELATION #8

You've already won the lottery.

Today is a fall on your knees, cry-tears-of-joy kind of day. Why? Because you are the recipient of an amazing dollop of good fortune, one you may not even be aware of.

Scientists have estimated the probability of you being born at about one in 400 trillion. Those odds are ten times greater than winning the Powerball and four thousand times greater than being hit by lightning. (As for winning the lottery and getting struck by lightning together? Our math skills don't reach that far.)

It turns out the amount of available DNA is so vast that the chance of it combining in the specific pattern to form the person you see in the mirror is *virtually impossible*. No scientific chance whatsoever. And yet, here you are.

The news gets more amazing — since those odds of one in 400 trillion against don't take into account the chance of your parents meeting, finding each other attractive, consummating their relationship, and having a single sperm and a single egg unite in joyous conception. We are now up to one in 400 quadrillion. (Even more if you add in surrogates.) In case you're wondering how big a quadrillion is, think of it as 1,000 trillions.

Are we finished? No, not yet. Factor your ancestors going back four billion years, all the variables that could have prevented them from ever meeting, dating, mating, and so on ...well, by the time you add up all the coincidences in this long tail scenario, the chances of you being here are one in ten to the power of 2,685,000. So the odds that you exist are basically zero. But because you do exist, and you're now aware of how precarious that is, you're the big winner today in the jackpot of life. Even if all you're doing right now is eating a chicken burrito with extra hot sauce.

What will you do with this knowledge? We suggest beginning each day with the understanding that you are a living, breathing phenomenon. Congratulations on that.

SECRET #206

What's in your sacred space?

Temples. Churches. Mosques. Zen centers. All qualify as sacred spaces. But so do the corner of your bedroom, a wall in your garden, or the passenger seat of your Toyota Celica — assuming you designate an area as a sanctuary and outfit it with objects of special significance to you. Ask yourself: What gives me joy? What makes me laugh? Why am I glad I'm currently a resident of Planet Earth? Then gather the objects, keepsakes and talismen that connect with your vision. Declare a spot "sacred" and place your incense, lucky bamboo and Mexican wrestler mask there. Create a ritual that goes with it. Bowing, kneeling, chanting mantras, humming your favorite Broadway show tune — all help elevate the spirit and generate good vibes, the kind of vibes that resonate far beyond the walls of your studio apartment, RV or yurt.

SECRET #153

Give yourself a gold star.

Society has bred us to be eager for acknowledgment from others. We work extra hard for the praise that comes from a job well done. And yet when one steps back from the daily striving, much of what we labor to accomplish is merely an illusion, as are the bon mots that come with it. When the boss says "Nice going!," does that overcome the inner suspicion that twelve hours spent finessing a PowerPoint presentation was a waste of time?

Don't rely on others to salute your effort. Give yourself props, and lots of them. For example, tomorrow when you wake up, if you make it out of bed, give yourself a gold star. And another one for brushing your teeth. And another for making yourself breakfast. This way, you'll be having a four-star day even before you leave the house.

Question: Why did Facebook create "likes" instead of gold stars? We recommend they change this to a more universally recognized system of praise.

SECRET #196

Exercise all face muscles.

Every time you smile, your brain releases neuropeptides to help lower stress. That alone would be worth the effort, but you also get a hit of dopamine and serotonin too. The more you practice smiling with your whole face involved — eyes, forehead, cheeks, the works — the more you'll naturally lift your spirits and those of everyone around you. Most importantly, if you can smile even in the worst of circumstances, then you're well on your way to mastering the key survival secret to life.

So don't hold back. Even if you feel like scowling, take the opposite tact. Show as many teeth as you can. See if the observer can count at least half your teeth when you beam at them. Don't worry if your choppers aren't Hollywood-ready. Many celebrities have incorporated their crooked smiles into eight-figure incomes. Kirsten Dunst, Steve Buscemi, and Ricky Gervais come to mind. No orthodontist would hold up their photos proudly, yet they're doing just fine. And even if you have poor dental hygiene, people will still return your smile (though they might back up a step or two).

For best results, we recommend brushing and flossing and visiting Dr. Kleinman twice a year.

PARABLE #3

Even Superman had super disappointments.

In 1938, the first true superhero comic book was born. The artist? Joseph "Joe" Shuster.

You might think that Joe lived a charmed existence after Superman became a hit. Instead, Joe's life was wrenched by a series of unforeseen tragedies, starting with selling his rights to the character for a mere $130.

Later, after Superman had become a household name, Joe and his writing partner tried to void their contract. No dice. Eventually after more legal hassles, the comic book company used others to create new Superman stories and removed Joe's name from the title altogether.

As you might guess, Joe's career headed south after that. Though he tried to create another smash hit, he couldn't find much traction with titles like *Funnyman* (a TV comedian becomes a superhero, using practical jokes to render criminals helpless). Eventually Joe's eyesight went bad, preventing him from drawing. He worked as a deliveryman to keep food on the table and moved in with his mother for a time. While a protest movement in the '70s forced DC Comics to restore his name to the Superman franchise and pony up a yearly stipend of $20,000, Joe fell into debt and died of congestive heart failure and hypertension.

So why is Joe's story one that a SuperOptimist can celebrate? Because he created what is arguably the most successful comic book character in history. Because he was a human being and made mistakes in areas that he wasn't skilled in, like reading fine print and engaging in corporate malfeasance. Because he had to deal with pain and suffering like we all do. Because many artists get ripped off during their lifetimes by corporate entities, and yet the white collar criminals who screwed Joe out of his creation will die in anonymity while Joe remains a true American hero!

This is Joe's original logo for the man of steel. It would grow more muscular as the character took off.

SECRET #179

Take the middle seat.

Having trouble focusing? Easily distracted? Diagnosed with ADD, ADHD, or DBD (Disruptive Behavior Disorder)? Let us help you get centered once and for all.

One way to accomplish this is to find the point in your body located just below the navel. In Qigong, it's called the "lower dantian." Concentrating on this central spot will help quiet your mind and allow you to deal with the task at hand.

Then again, maybe you need a bigger shock to your system. In that case, pack a satchel, jump in the car and head to Lebanon, Kansas, the geographical center of the continental United States. Just take US Highway 281 north one mile and turn west on K-191. Go for another mile until you see the marker at the end of the road.* Sign the guest register, have a seat, and luxuriate in the great expanse that is the Sunflower State. There's very little to do once you get here. And isn't that the point? Just think: now nobody's more centered than you.

**The actual geographical center of the country is a short walk away, in the middle of a former hog farm.*

SECRET #122

Your mathematical constant.

Choosing a number that has sacred meaning for you can be invaluable for daily challenges, like deciding what PIN to program into your ATM card. For your number, you may want to reflect on the best year of your life thus far or ask a numerologist to suggest a hot integer. Then again, you could just pick a number out of a hat and immediately tattoo it on your chest in a sign of "letting go."

Consider the number four (4). While some might not think it remarkable, it is sacred to the Zia Indians, as this digit embodies the powers of nature — the four directions of east, west, north, and south, the seasons, and the ages of man. Four was also Lou Gehrig's number, as The Iron Horse helped power the Yankees to six world championships while hitting .340 lifetime (sans steroids).

Of course, the Chinese would disagree. Four is a dreaded number in their view. This is because it sounds similar to the Chinese word "si" which means "death." Gehrig succumbed to amyotrophic lateral sclerosis at age thirty-seven, so they might have a point.

One you determine which number speaks to you most, write it down and place it in your wallet for easy referral. When asked how many silver dollar flapjacks you want at breakfast, it's a no-brainer. You can also use it to customize your license plate, have it monogrammed on your dress shirts, or legally change your name to it, as our friend Ms. Eight Zero Five did.

May your special number bring you joy and prove beneficial in all areas of life.

Maybe this is the one.

SECRET #124

Stop and smell everything.

Walter Hagen was neither a spiritual healer nor self-help author, but a major figure in the sport of golf. His winning ways ushered in a world of riches for professional athletes, as he became the first to earn a million dollars playing a sport for a living.*

But we honor him not for his ways with a five iron, but for his ability to appreciate the moment. “You’re only here for a short visit," Hagen said. "Don’t hurry, don’t worry. And be sure to smell the flowers along the way.”

Notice Hagen didn’t just choose roses to sniff. Jasmine, hyacinth, peony, wisteria: each deserves our undivided attention. But why limit one's olfactory sense to flowers? To be truly awake and in the moment, we suggest you take a good whiff of everything that crosses your path.

While a fresh-baked cherry pie cooling at the window of Aunt Millicent’s kitchen or that sweet huff of unleaded gasoline at the Exxon station are in our top ten smells of all time, we focus our nose on the questionable smells too. Like a New York subway platform on a hot summer day, rotting fish left out to wither in the sun at the seafood market, even a freshly minted poop from a beloved labradoodle. Such smells wake us up to the moment and should not be pushed away just because we find them off-putting. They’re as valuable in our ongoing education as the waft of evergreens in a forest or the scent of recently-mowed grass.

And speaking of labradoodles, you might notice just how eager they are to smell the world, whether it be a pant leg, a tree trunk, or a Goodyear steel-belted radial. Like all dogs, they possess up to 300 million olfactory receptors in their nose, compared to a mere six million in humans. And the part of a dog's brain that is devoted to analyzing smells is, proportionally speaking, forty times greater than ours. No wonder the police are always walking dogs around the airport in search of the odd bag of cocaine.

So take your olfactory senses for a walk and get a whiff of everything. One note: When sniffing fellow humans, be discreet. Some take offense if you get too close, even though it's only natural.

**Hagen once stated that he "never wanted to be a millionaire, just to live like one." A fortunate man, he achieved both.*

SECRET #180

Yawn like a leader.

Some consider a public yawn to be a sign of poor manners. Nonsense. Your yawn actually indicates that you are deep thinker, a hard worker, and dare we say, a luminary in your field. Here's why:

Scientists at Princeton University postulate that yawning plays a vital role in your well-being by cooling your brain. When you start to yawn, the stretching of the jaw increases blood flow to your cranium, while forcing the downward flow of spinal fluid. Air breathed into the mouth during the yawn chills these fluids, like a car's radiator cooling the engine.

The next time you feel a yawn coming on, don't stifle it, nor hide it behind a hand or elbow. Let your yawn announce itself, jaws agape, eyes clenched shut, arms stretched to the sky. Whatever sound that arises within the cave-like expanse of your mouth, let it echo as if it were a note ringing out from the stage of the Metropolitan Opera.

End your yawn with a satisfying sigh and a smack of the lips. Should anyone ask why you're taking so much pleasure in the act, explain to them the science behind the activity. Of course you're yawning. You're simply cooling your brain off, since it has been working overtime. Suggest to them that the reason they're not yawning is because they don't have as many world-changing ideas as you. Watch as they suddenly follow your lead and start yawning like crazy.

You are a leader. A leader of yawns. Now isn't that satisfying?

A yawn worthy of respect.

SECRET #136

Feeling depressed? Try Nevada.

Of all fifty states in the union, only Nevada showed a decline in its suicide rate according to a recent survey. To what can we attribute this positive development amid the collective angst being experienced in the U.S.? Could it be the easy access to casinos? The legalized prostitution? Well, sure! But there's more. We've done some informal research, and among the advantages to bringing one's particular personality disorder to Nevada are the following:

1. No state income tax.
2. 300 sunny days a year.
3. Short winters.
4. Beautiful scenery.
5. World class skiing.
6. Las Vegas Aviators minor league baseball.
7. Cheap flights in and out.
8. Legal marijuana.
9. Good stargazing.
10. Second highest percentage of UFO sightings in the country.

11. No fault divorce laws.

12. Burning Man nearby.

13. Snickers bars made here.

Feeling better now? Just remember, if you do move to the Silver State, you need to pronounce the name correctly. It's Nev–AD–uh, not Nev-AH-duh. See you there!

Note: Nevada schools rank dead last in the nation. So don't come looking to raise your IQ or hoping your children will become Rhodes Scholars. On the plus side, if you're a good teacher you can really make a difference here.

BATTING TIP #1

Fear strikes out.

Babe Ruth didn't let the naysayers prevent him from approaching the plate with a swagger and a smile. Yet plenty of people wanted to see him fail and fail he did. Not only was the Babe called the "Sultan of Swat," he was also known as the "King of Strikeouts." In fact, he led the American League in whiffs five times and accumulated 1,330 of them in his career. If he had been afraid of getting beaten at the plate, he never would have launched 714 dingers over the outfield fence.

"Never let the fear of striking out get in your way," Ruth famously said. So take a tip from the Colossus of Clout — dare to fail and laugh about it when you do. Then get back in the batter's box and see what happens next.*

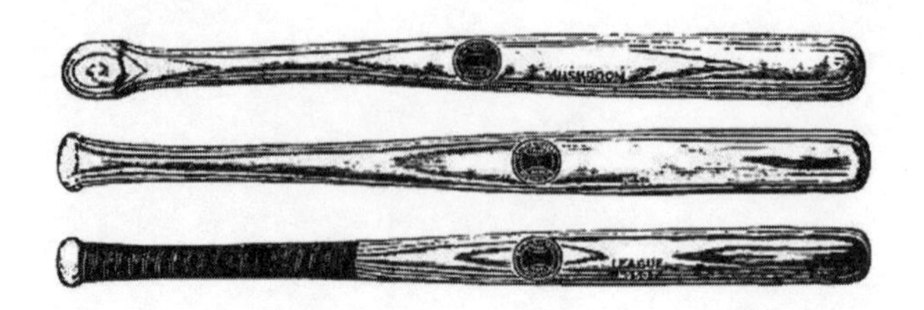

**Should you knock one out of the park, be prepared for chin music from the opposing pitcher on your next turn at the plate.*

SECRET #125

Think like a Martian.

What if you weren't confined to normal, everyday thoughts? Maybe you'd be more likely to do something dangerous or extraordinary.

Take Elon Musk: he spent $100 million dollars of his own money developing rocket technology aimed at colonizing Mars. Better yet, he convinced his friends and the U.S. government to contribute an additional $900 million to help build his new generation of SpaceX rockets.

Is Elon crazy? Yes. Will he get to Mars? Also yes. There is no stopping Elon. Which reminds us that before you can do something amazing, you have to leave all the dull Earthly rules and restrictions behind. You have to think like a Martian. When you look at life fresh, like you've never seen it before, you're liable to conjure some pretty way-out ideas. Who knows what might come of them?

SECRET #183

Heads you win. Tails you also win.

Lots of people play it safe as they age, and for good reason. "Safe" seems to be a wiser choice than "sorry." But could it be that we actually have this backwards?

Adhering to a predetermined routine means you know pretty much what each day is going to bring, even before you live it. In the meantime, the world around you is constantly changing, so the safe path may be more uncertain than you think.

How do you prevent yourself from becoming ossified? We recommend adding two risks a week into your calendar. To start, try those with a relatively high probability of success. Forgo the usual grape jelly and make yourself a peanut butter and honey sandwich instead. Break the pattern and stroll down a different block on your way to town. Turn off CNN and watch a video that offers insight into the history of Japan.

Getting the hang of it? Now you're ready to double down on risk, where your adrenals kick up a notch. Take a week's wages and visit the nearest casino for a few spins of the roulette wheel. You could win enough to pay off your mortgage — or find yourself without money for the grocery tab. Audition for an off-off Broadway show, despite your lack of acting experience. Your long shot might pay off in a featured role, or you could be driven from the theater with catcalls and brickbats. Approach a stranger and say hello. It could spark a new friendship. Or maybe not.

No matter what happens, the chance of you coming out on top is 100%. Win or lose, succeed or stumble, you get to face your fears, collect more information for the next time, and have a swell story to tell your friends back at the salad bar, water cooler, or book club (where they're doing exactly what they did yesterday — but not you).

Pas de risque, pas de récompense.

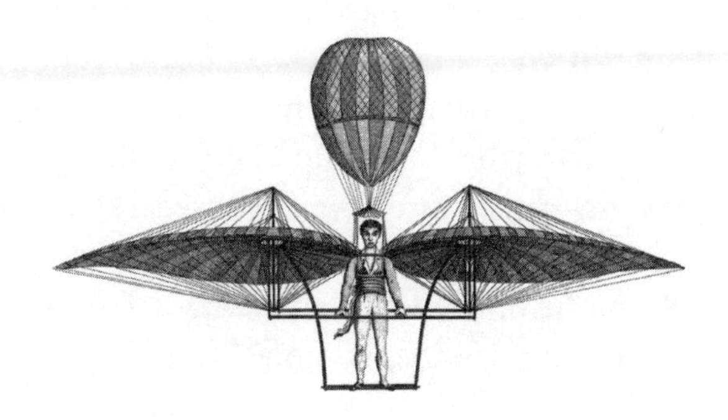

Gradually work your way up to this.

SECRET #119

Cheer up, it's Monday.

It's perfectly natural to curse "the worst day of the week." But we're here to tell you it's not the 24 hours you've been conditioned to believe.

Monday has a great deal going for it. First off, you've probably stored up a few more winks thanks to "no alarm Saturday" and "slept through church Sunday." Plus two days away from the office is a restorative in itself. That's good, solid energy you can draw upon. Then there are the remarkable stories you can spill to your work mates regarding your blissed-out triumph of a weekend, like how you rolled sevens at the World Dice Championship. (Remember, everyone exaggerates his or her own adventures. Feel free to do the same.) Finally, Monday gives you the perfect excuse to drag your heels a bit before you tackle that inbox full of projects, deadlines, and gut-clenching notes from your churlish supervisor.

If you really want to bitch about a day, try Tuesday. That's when the work has backed up, the boss is getting testy, and the real poo-poo hits the fan. Yep, Tuesday's the day you're most likely to work through your lunch break due to the realization that you screwed around on Monday, and now you're behind the 8-ball.

So rather than assume that Monday is going to be an ungodly descent into Hades, why not look at the facts. And then enjoy showing people your pictures from that Saturday evening rave, where the cops arrested everyone but you. Have a swell Monday. You've earned it.

Nearly one in five employees will leave the office late on a Tuesday as they try to play catch up.

REVELATION #5

Good news about bed bugs.

People freak out over bed bugs to a degree that's not warranted. These aren't like having a deadly whistling spider in your bed, or waking up to a mound of fire ants making a meal of your torso.

First off, it doesn't hurt when a bed bug sucks your blood. And while bed bugs can harbor various pathogens, transmission to humans has not been proven and is considered unlikely, as any medical professional will tell you. And sure, it's a bit of a nuisance to get rid of the pesky creatures. But look at the positive side. It will force you to clean so you'll be all caught up on laundry. And you'll be motivated to get rid of some of the clutter that can serve as a bed for the bugs so aptly named. Are you listening, Marie Kondo?

What's more, getting rid of bed bugs will also eliminate non-target pests, like spiders and ants and maybe centipedes too. So while it may suck (literally) to discover bed bugs in your home or office, we're here to tell you that things could be worse. For one thing, you could have scabies. There, don't you feel better now?

If someone calls you a "bed bug," don't take it so hard. If someone calls you a "Formosan termite," that could be something to get worked up about.

REVELATION #4

You are better than LeBron James.

LeBron James is six foot nine and a superior athlete. He's also a good businessman and an intriguing celebrity. He earns a ton of dollars, gets feted at awards banquets, and is lavished with the trappings of a king (which happens to be his nickname).

Society may want to rob you of your superiority to Mr. James by placing him on a pedestal. And yet, *you are better than LeBron James*. Even if his physical coordination is so uncanny that he could carry a teacup on his head through a hurricane.

The fact is, you're the only you that exists on this planet, which counts for a lot. LeBron knows that size and athletic talent is not the secret of his success. It's motivation. As James himself notes, "Greatness is defined by how much you want to put into what you do." So while you might not be able to jump as high as LeBron, your motivation and desire have no physical limitations. The sky's the limit.

Besides, right now LeBron James may have already come down from last night's victory and is dealing with some petty legal matter or pesky interview request, while you're able to wander outside and enjoy a plate of crinkle-cut French fries. Who's got it better now?

So up your game today. The sooner you look yourself in the mirror and say, "Damnit, LeBron James has nothing on me," the sooner you'll start receiving compliments on your improved posture and confident demeanor. You may even school LeBron in your particular field of endeavor and show him what real success looks like. And you can share your fries with him, if you are the magnanimous sort.

Note: You can substitute any athlete, celebrity or captain of industry for this exercise and it still works.

SECRET #133

High knee lift step.

There's nothing quite like a drum and bugle corps playing John Philip Sousa at the volume of a jet turbine to get the blood flowing. Even a single snare being smacked in 4/4 time will motivate toe-tapping in those under heavy sedation.

Depending on your affinity for marching bands, we suggest you acquire a second-hand bass drum, then ask a few neighbors to take their tubas and xylophones out of mothballs. Begin with some simple exercises, then work your way up to "Stars and Stripes Forever."* Among the many benefits you'll accrue from taking up this practice:

a. Positive team spirit among band members.

b. Meeting the challenge of marching at one tempo while playing at another, enhancing your neuronal connections and increasing your ability to multi-task in a variety of situations.

c. Heightened body awareness from marching backwards and sideways while facing straight ahead, ensuring you have a good sense of where you are in space and aiding your balance.

**For those who don't join in, noise-cancelling headphones make a great gift.*

SECRET #201

Avoid the explanation.

"Explain why you decided to walk across the United States barefoot."

"Explain why you spent ten years by yourself in a Nepalese cave."

"Explain what motivated you to jump your motorcycle over the Snake River Canyon."

The world is filled with bystanders who question the event but who do not take part. Also known as onlookers, gawkers, or rubberneckers, they can be seen with jaws agape as a circus performer eats glass, a diver leaps from a 200-meter springboard, or a pianist sets fire to his instrument before commencing his performance.

Everybody on the sidelines wants to hear another story. And they want to know why the person undertook an activity that stretched beyond the norm. That's why there are gossip columnists, cable news anchors and prison wardens. Forget the explanations and just keep jumping off your own metaphorical high dive. Let your work — or your inactivity — speak for itself.

SECRET #141

Your celebrity friends.

Denzel Washington. Lionel Messi. Awkwafina.

Everyone can benefit from claiming a celebrity as a close personal acquaintance, especially during a slow point in a conversation or when negotiating for a bank loan. There's not a person in the world who isn't impressed when you're tight with somebody famous.

Whether you really know the person is of no importance. What makes it work is your conviction that this person would be your best pal if, in fact, they did know you. Pick a well-known figure: Pope Francis, Channing Tatum, Rihanna. Who knows? The more you concentrate on the fantasy relationship, the more it might actually come true.

Bonus points: Retouch yourself into a photograph with your celebrity pal so you have proof that this relationship is powerful and legitimate.

SECRET #162

Pain? Illness? Hair loss? Snake oil to the rescue.

Anybody who tries to sell us a miracle cure for what ails us is more often a cheat then a savior. But is that fair assessment of snake oil salesmen? Not necessarily.

Assuming you're using the authentic formula derived from the fat of the Chinese water snake, snake oil does have measurable health effects. The oil possesses a high level of eicosapentaenoic acid (EPA) directly linked to a number of benefits for human health, like loosening up stiff joints and relieving inflammation. It also has analgesic properties which makes it a popular balm following surgery, or during a chronic illness. Used as a rub, this oil can speed up healing of wounds and injuries.

Not only that, if you find yourself losing your temper without a good explanation, rub a small amount of snake oil on your temples or apply it to your chest and feel your mood improve. And don't forget the scalp in order to prevent hair from falling out.

Caveat emptor: There are plenty of snakes in the world, but their venom doesn't contain the level of EPA that will help cure your ills. American patent-medicine peddlers of the late 1900's sold liniments labeled "rattlesnake oil", but the oil of rattlesnakes has 1/10th the level of active ingredient compared to that of the Chinese water snake.

Since 1400 BC, the Caduceus has been the symbol for medical professionals. Considering it features two Aesculapian snakes, that can't be an accident.

SECRET #175

Choose a spirit animal. Walk it regularly.

Dogs and cats are fine as pets. But do they embody your own characteristics as much as, say, a sea lion? Or an osprey?

In the Native American tradition, picking a spirit animal with deep connection to your being will help guide you as you go forward. For example, by claiming the owl as your totem, you've picked a symbol with deep sagacity, not to mention "gut instinct." With the owl by your side, your ability to see what's hidden to others will flourish. Let the owl guide you beyond illusion and deceit to the true reality. But don't flinch; often this reality isn't what we've been led to believe by our teachers, clergy, or local news outlets.

In addition, if you're ready to explore the unknown with its potential for mystery and magic, the owl offers the courage necessary to venture into a parallel universe without fear. Do you have a spirit animal? If not, the owl is a very wise choice.

Stare at this owl rendering and you'll soon absorb the intuitive knowledge that will keep you awake, alert and in touch with what's really going on. Especially at night.

SECRET #148

Embrace the Dunning-Kruger effect.

People who have virtually no skill in something often rate themselves as near experts. Why? Because they have no idea how much they don't know, and how much they still have to learn.

Ignorance is, in fact, a blissful state; a theory proven by social psychologists David Dunning and Justin Kruger in their landmark study. While the Dunning-Kruger effect might be something to avoid if you're interested in becoming a thoracic surgeon, industrial architect, or Supreme Court justice, for the rest of us, embracing a lack of "structured learning" may lead to fresh and exciting work.

Buddhists strive for this kind of openness to life, minus judgment or criticism, calling it "beginner's mind." They practice detachment from thought in order to experience each moment with a fresh perspective. Picasso himself said that it took him four years to paint like Raphael but a lifetime to paint like a child. Enjoying a bit of "illusory superiority" can't hurt if you're wielding a brush or writing a poem.*

**Though the opposite is true if you're operating a forty-story construction crane or facing your thesis examination committee at MIT.*

PARABLE #2

Danger vs. opportunity.

It was a risky move in 1972 when President Richard M. Nixon decided to make cordial overtures to the People's Republic of China. The U.S. had been at odds with the Asia-Pacific country since 1949, when Mao Zedong took over leadership of China's communist party. Despite decades of chilly relations, Nixon decided to warm things up and made a visit to Beijing to meet elder statesman Mao. This began a normalization process that resumed relations between the two countries and helped drive a wedge between China and the Soviet Union. Nixon said about his trip: "The Chinese use two brush strokes to write the word crisis. One brush stroke stands for danger; the other for opportunity. In a crisis, be aware of the danger -- but recognize the opportunity." Wise words indeed.

A symbol that incorporates both danger and opportunity will look good on the back of your motorcycle jacket.

SECRET #120

Go for the pure oxygen.

Ever hear of George Yantz? Born in Louisville, Kentucky, George was a professional baseball player whose big league career consisted of one major league game. He only made it to The Show for a "cup of coffee," a very brief stint that sometimes only lasts a single at bat. In fact, of the 18,000 or so players (and counting) who've run up the dugout steps and onto an MLB field, 974 have had one-game careers.

Some might say it's a tragedy that the fates allowed George only the briefest of glimpses before he was sent packing. And yet, how many of us would give half their 401Ks to be able to say we had been a major leaguer at one point in our lives?

So even if you're like George and have the shortest of stints at the top, and are summarily replaced by someone younger and nimbler than you, take pride in that one gulp of pure oxygen. You might just appreciate the experience more than Babe Ruth, Hank Aaron and Pete Rose combined. And people will continue to buy you coffee (or something stronger) just to hear you recount the one time you stood at the plate facing high heat.

George was able to say he hit an astounding 1.000 for his career, going 1 for 1 with a single on the one day he played. September 30, 1912. You could look it up.

SECRET #155

Enjoy your pickle.

Founding father Thomas Jefferson once wrote: "On a hot day in Virginia, I know nothing more comforting than a fine spiced pickle, brought up trout-like from the sparkling depths of the aromatic jar below the stairs of Aunt Sally's cellar."

Another big fan of the pickle? Jefferson's buddy George, who cultivated and collected both rare and commonplace plants in the gardens at Mount Vernon. America's first president amassed a whopping collection of 476 different varieties of cucumbers meant for pickling.

The moral of this story? If you have a very deep and powerful enthusiasm for something — even as common as a pickle — follow your interest as far as it will go. Let your passion fully flower. It may lead to a lot more than just a tasty pickle; you might just start a country as dandy as the U.S.A.

SECRET #174

Complaining is good for you.

Popular opinion would like you to believe that unfettered positivity is the key to a happy, successful life. But what if these cheerful idiots are wrong?

As with most blanket pronouncements, their claim of constant conviviality is utter nonsense. Complaining is like perspiring. It's part of human nature, and a necessary outlet for dealing with the stresses and strains of mortality. Life is challenging, whether you're a trash collector attempting to wake up at 4 a.m. for your Thursday shift or Nicole Kidman working hard to cling to the top of the Hollywood pecking order despite her age.

If you feel guilty for not being constantly "happy" or "well-adjusted," you have our permission to stop right now and let out a good, long sigh, followed by a string of choice expletives. Give yourself license to let off some steam.* Otherwise, when things really do go off the rails in your life, you won't have the tools to deal with the problem successfully.

**Of course, constant whining can cause your friends and family to evade your presence. Mix it up a little by adding self-effacing humor to your litany of problems. They'll thank you for it.*

SECRET #119

Attempt a world record.

Concerned your obituary will read like a boilerplate legal document? We suggest trying to get your name in the record books pronto.

A sure-fire way to be acknowledged is to set a goal that others have ignored. For world-class athletes like sprinter Usain Bolt and tight-rope walkers like Nik Wallenda, attempting to break a new world record in their respective fields requires intense training and unwavering focus. Lucky for the rest of us, there are hundreds of less glamorous records out there begging to be broken.

How about "most T-shirts worn at one time" (current record: 260). Most tennis balls held in one hand (27). Fastest time to assemble a Mr. Potato Head while blindfolded (14.90 seconds). Fastest time to duct tape a person to a wall (26.69 seconds). Most pieces of pumpkin pie eaten in ten minutes (50, or 17.5 lbs. of pie).

Better yet, make up your own amazing feat to astound and delight.* After all, world records start with envisioning the impossible and then determining that you can overcome the odds.

**Do it on wheels and raise the difficulty level by a factor of seven.*

PARABLE #1

"Mess" rhymes with "success."

The world knows Barbara Bush as the former wife of the 41st U.S. president and mother of the 43rd. In those roles, she had to be stalwart in the face of public pressure and criticism. She faced heavy scrutiny inside and outside the White House.

But behind closed doors, Babs knew how to let herself go. Her attitude towards perfectionism? As she stated, "The darn trouble with cleaning the house is it gets dirty the next day anyway. So skip a week if you have to." If B.B. could overcome society's push towards having everything neat and tidy —which life never is — then so can we. This includes eating turnips, meeting deadlines, and returning phone calls from the IRS. We applaud her for turning her back on such small-minded thinking — as well as not dying her hair or getting any Botox (that we know of).

As for her politics, Babs said, "I don't like attacking." So we'll leave it at that.

SECRET #149

Tough day? Consider the seahorse.

Here's a reason to feel fortunate: At least you're not a small marine fish in the genus Hippocampus.

Despite living in salt water, far from the stress of major urban areas, only five in a thousand seahorses survive to adulthood. While there are many reasons for their short life span, swimming upright using only a dorsal fin could cause anyone to expire early.

Their shape and body type also make them one of the slowest-moving fish in the world, so they're easy prey for Asian fishermen eager to supply the marketplace. (In China, they're prescribed for impotence, wheezing, nocturnal enuresis, and pain, though no clinical studies have been performed to validate these cures.)

All things considered, it's lucky you're not checking the clock every five seconds like the seahorse to see if your time's up.

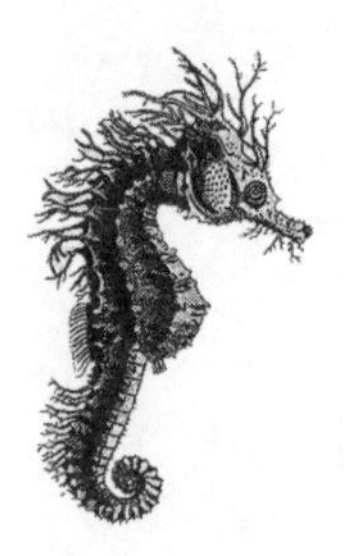

SECRET #142

Open doors for others.
Walk through them yourself.

If you find it getting stuffy in your home, office, car or — most especially — cranium, take a cue from Aldous Huxley and expand your mind.

Now we're not advocating taking drugs to alter your perceptions. Rather, we recommend opening the nearest door, walking out of the confines you are currently in and towards a meditation center, nature preserve, or art studio.* All are more genuine ways of breaking through to the other side, without the nasty side effects.

As Aldous said, “The ordinary waking consciousness... is by no means the only form of consciousness, nor in all circumstances the best. Insofar as he transcends his ordinary self and his ordinary mode of awareness, the mystic is able to enlarge his vision, to look more deeply into the unfathomable miracle of existence.”

**Huxley himself began practicing meditation years before he experimented with substances.*

SECRET #127-A

The wonderful conclusion that everything's already been done (part one).

All the stories in the universe may boil down to the following premises: 1. David vs. Goliath 2. The Odd Couple. Both have been done to death and will continue to be until the earth is destroyed by a cataclysmic event, which will be the ultimate Odd Couple story.

So sit back, relax, and let the knowledge that everything's been done give you a comfortable, easy-chair feeling. Why, even the iPod is just a Walkman with semiconductors, and the Walkman was just a portable Harman/Kardon stereo with headphones, and the stereo came from mono, and mono came from 78s, and 78s came from Thomas Edison's phonograph, and the phonograph came from some poor guy who let Edison see it one day and then Edison stole the idea...the pattern is obvious.

"It's all been done before; therefore I don't have all the pressure on me" is the SuperOptimist view. "It's all been done before, therefore I'll just artfully pre-select what's been done, reorder and reshape it, and then call it my own" is another. This was the favorite of William Burroughs, author of "Naked Lunch," who clipped words, sentences and paragraphs from other books, then pasted them together to form a new work of art. He was just cutting to the chase so he could spend more time on his true avocation, which was being a junkie.

So tap into the Doneness of the Universe and see where it leads you. David and Goliath? Or the Odd Couple? What about "The Odd Couple vs. David and Goliath?" You're already on your way to success with that kind of thinking.

SECRET #127-B

The wonderful conclusion that everything's already been done (part two).

Whether it's writing, painting, or opening a kebab stand, conventional wisdom implores you to "find your own voice." But is that really necessary? Maybe instead of driving yourself mad chasing after that invisible ghost known as "originality," you should just get busy copying the people you admire most.

That's what Ray LaMontagne did. Before he was a famous musician, he was just another schlub working a dead-end job in a Maine shoe factory, with no prospects other than surviving another shift. Then one morning he awoke to his clock radio playing Stephen Stills' "Treetop Flyer." For reasons known only to the gods, the clock radio, and Ray, instead of reporting for work that day, he decided to become a singer-songwriter himself.

With what little money he had, he bought a bunch of old records by Bob Dylan, Joni Mitchell and The Big O, Otis Redding, and began slavishly imitating them. He basically holed up in his apartment for a couple of years and let Redding be his guide. By transmitting The King of Soul's voice through his own larynx, he developed a skill set that eventually led him to multi-platinum recording success.

In other words, Ray found his own voice by borrowing someone else's. So if you want to make a splash, do the following: 1) Quit your job. 2) Tell your friends you'll be unreachable for a while. 3) Immerse yourself in the work of your favorite pop star, business tycoon or squash champion* until you can repeat it from memory.

Whatever your pursuit, it won't be long before your mind alters its circuitry based on the information being fed into it. You'll still be processing it through your own passageways, so what comes out on the other side will be considered original — unless your goal is to be a Lady Gaga impersonator.

How long will it take for you to hit the big time? If you're a fast learner, give it about five years. And then, when you become a raging success,** be like Ray and admit your thieving ways without shame. There are no original voices. And isn't that a relief?

**To master the sport of squash, start by watching all the videos of Mohamed Elshorbagy you can find. Gluing a racquet to your hand is also advised.*

***Notice we didn't say "if". This is SuperOptimism, after all.*

SECRET #151

The news is better in French.

As human beings, we like to be kept company by voices other than our own. So we switch on various devices for stories of the day. Yet the sounds of the media often exacerbate worry and strife, especially in times of crisis. That's why we recommend listening to the latest programming in a foreign language; one you can't comprehend.* When you remove the brain's desire to process and understand each word, you can relax and appreciate the sounds on their own.

On a different planet, these sounds could be coming from aliens. In the spirit world, they could be shamans speaking in tongues. It's akin to experimental music, or abstract painting. Let your imagination conjure its own story about what these voices are talking about. Being stuck in an elevator? Ligue 1 Football? Cooking pastry?

To pick up the signal, we recommend a nice shortwave radio, one that also doubles as an emergency transponder should the need arise. Hand-cranked and solar powered, it never needs batteries or electricity and can receive signals from as far away as Siberia. And should you prefer a different tongue than la belle langue française, you'll find plenty of stations in Spanish, along with Russian, Arabic, Chinese, Polish — even Creole.

**After listening for a month or two, you may pick up enough meaning in the words to consider yourself bilingual.*

SECRET #202

Comfort is slavery.

Comfort doesn't motivate personal growth, discomfort does. So don't try to distance yourself from misfortune. See what you can make from a bad grade, crap assignment, or shattered dream. Suddenly, you're able to feel at ease even when a shit storm arrives. Then every lost wallet, dropped phone call, job dismissal, and broken bone will lose its ability to disrupt your life. How welcome is that?

Try wearing one of these at the office and see if you don't experience personal growth instantly.

SECRET #134

The benefits of freaking out.

In the early 1960s, former marathon dancing champion Vito Paulekas and his wife Szou established an art studio and boutique in Hollywood. It fast became the epicenter of a new movement combining semi-communal living with free-form dancing. They called themselves “freaks” or “freakers” and became known in the area for their unconventional behavior. Among those who congregated at Paulekas’ place were Frank Zappa, Don Van Vliet, and The GTOs.

It was Zappa, leader of the seminal '60s group The Mothers of Invention, who described their behavior thusly: “Freaking out is a process whereby an individual casts off outmoded and restricted standards of thinking, dress and social etiquette in order to express creatively his relationship to his environment and the social structure as a whole.” It’s no surprise that Zappa’s first album with The Mothers was entitled *Freak Out*. It also happened to be the first double album debut in history, which was a freaky thing to do.

To let one's "freak flag fly” now means any sort of fun, mischief or invention that can be had at the expense of normality. We invite you to get up from your desk, walk outside and express yourself however you please. See how good it feels. Just make sure no one from Human Resources is nearby.*

**The folks in HR don’t let their freak flags fly until they’re at home with the shades drawn.*

SECRET #181

Disobey that which needs disobeying.

On June 7, 1893, a young Indian lawyer was asked to vacate the first-class compartment of a train because he was not white-skinned. He refused and told the railway officers that he would not go voluntarily; they would have to throw him out.* The act of standing up against injustice was, in effect, Mahatma Gandhi's first act of civil disobedience. It's always a good day to channel the spirit of this activist to promote people's rights — and independent thinking besides.

**He got what he asked for. Gandhi was tossed from the compartment and his luggage was flung out too. The train sped away, leaving him freezing outside the station. However, he didn't lose his front teeth in this encounter. That came later.*

SECRET #150

The only competition worth winning.

It's clear that humans like creating contests — and picking winners. There are a huge number of competitions ranging from small local prizes to large international Grands Prix, for everything from portrait painting to sandcastle building, with stuffy judges deciding who is "better" and who is "worse."

People can go batshit crazy comparing themselves to other people. Rather than get caught up in this unfulfilling exercise, try the only competition that makes sense — the internal competition with yourself. Look at what you were doing five years ago and see if you've made any progress. If you do an honest analysis and have made no progress towards better work in the last five years - great! This realization means your progress can start today. Experiment with a new style or process. Go off the map into the unknown, even if it means taking a turn down a mysterious dark highway and ending up with one last $10 chip in a Northern California casino.

Here's how Mr. David Jones (nee Bowie) framed it: "... if you feel safe in the area you're working in, you're not working in the right area. Always go a little further into the water than you feel you're capable of being in. Go a little bit out of your depth, and when you don't feel that your feet are quite touching the bottom, you're just about in the right place to do something exciting."

Are your feet touching the bottom? Wade out further. Now isn't that better?

If you'd like more recognition for your efforts, we recommend purchasing a trophy for yourself. The bigger, the better. When anyone asks how you got it, you can tell them "I'm a winner at life." Who can argue with that?

SECRET #123

Put a lid on it.

Every day of every annum now constitutes a celebration of sorts. Surely you're aware of National Corn Chip Day, National Personal Trainer Awareness Day, and National Static Electricity Day? But we can think of no day we enjoy more than January 15th — National Hat Day.

Perhaps it's because we tend towards the pragmatic, but wearing a hat seems to make a lot of sense (especially when it's cold outside). But we also like how this holiday jars us from casual wear to reach in the closet for something special.

While there are many choices, from Stetsons to pith helmets to feathered French chapeaus, here we highlight the fez for your consideration. A felt headdress in the shape of a short cylinder, it is named after the city Fez, the kingdom of Morocco until 1927. Because of its impractical nature (as a topper for soldiers, it made the head a target for enemy fire and provided little protection from the sun), the fez was relegated over the years to ceremonial wear and was taken up by various fraternal organizations, among them the Shriners, whom we admire for their ability to fit into tiny automobiles.

While we will proudly sport our fez, rest assured it will be indoors, as we have no intention of chasing a blowing lid down 8th Avenue. Here's to National Hat Day. We doff our caps to you.

By some counts, there are over 1,500 national days of commemoration in the calendar. As for SuperOptimist Day? We're in celebratory mode 24/7/365.

SECRET #147

The fountain of youth, revealed.

While scientists work on reverse-engineering your molecular clock to match that of the ageless jellyfish, you've still got to deal with your bum ankle, your stiff neck, and that odd swelling on your right index finger.

So what's the answer to the burden of aging? To really shed the heavy weight of the years, we advise tapping into the energy of your own mad spirit and childlike nature. We call this "The Power of Immaturity" and it promises to rejuvenate you as well as any miracle drug. Here are a few suggestions to ignite your consciousness like a Roman candle:

Ride your bicycle somewhere new. Remember when you were young? You'd get on your three-speed and race around the block. That block seemed like a trip around the world because everything was fresh and you were an explorer to rival both Lewis and Clark. Why not kick start your sense of wonder today by pedaling to an unfamiliar location. Exposing yourself to the new will induce plasticity in your brain, which is where kids have it all over adults. It can be as simple as heading down a side street or as drastic as putting a "for sale" sign on your house, packing a satchel and heading out into the great wide open.

Remove preconceptions one by one. The plaque that's built up around your emotional state? It's called "familiarity" and there's a reason it breeds contempt. Kids have an innate sense of wonder because they haven't seen it all. It's true you've got a lot of miles on your odometer, but you can still wipe your slate clean with what Buddhists call *Shoshin.* It takes practice to greet another day with an attitude that's eager for new experiences. But once you get the hang of it, you can employ it at will.

Do not put away childish things. While 1 Corinthians 13 in the Bible talks about doing away with the trappings of youth, the Apostle Paul was referring to becoming a generous, loving person, not about throwing away your Batman comic books, or jettisoning your K-pop albums, or turning away from the horror movies you loved when you were ten. Keep a drawer filled with the items that fascinated you when you didn't have so many rings on your tree, to act as talismans and help you conjure the great power of your youth.

Whatever you think you're too old to do now, do it. How many crazy chances did you take as a kid? Some of them worked out. Some left you with major contusions. That you made it to adulthood really flies in the face of common sense. Really, you've been granted extra time on earth. Don't waste it trying to play it safe now. Do something that people will scoff at. Let them admonish you for "not acting your age." They are mere fossils, not a living, breathing Triceratops like you.

SECRET #157

Partner with a weirdo.

Maybe they don't make pleasant chitchat before the meeting. Maybe they look at you funny and you're a little scared of them. Maybe they don't sugarcoat things with friendly banter. But the edge-dwelling, unpredictable wildcards with their social awkwardness, strange ticks, and disdain for niceties? They're the ones that trigger the innovations necessary for progress.

Inside they're teeming with ideas, both constructive and destructive. Sometimes the destructive ones can lead to completely dismantling a failing enterprise and driving towards a fresh, modern way of thinking. You never know unless you ask the oddball to step forward and give you their "honest assessment."

Call them misfits, nerds, sociopaths (hopefully minus any violent tendencies). But whatever you do, don't call them out for being different than you. Get them on your side by not judging their flakiness as a "bad thing." Chances are, when you examine yourself in light of their behavior, you will often find that you're just as weird as they are.

If their answer to your latest question is to scribble this on the wall, don't dismiss it out of hand. Spend some time examining it; you may be surprised at what emerges.

SECRET #171

This could be the day you meet someone new.

That's what happened to a guy named Paul.

A friend of his from high school invited him to come check out a band playing at a local church. He could have said no, but he didn't. And if he had only shaken hands with Eric Griffiths (guitar), Colin Hanton (drums), Rod Davies (banjo), Pete Shotton (washboard) or Len Garry (tea chest bass), then history wouldn't have been written.

But he focused on the guy leading the band. "He was singing 'Come Go With Me,' the Del-Vikings' song, which I thought was fabulous until I realized they weren't the right words," recalled Paul. "He was changing them. 'Come go with me ... down to the penitentiary' — he was nicking folk-song words and chain-gang words and putting them into the Del-Vikings' songs, a clever little bit of ingenuity."

Why not take a cue from Paul and venture outside to meet someone new? Who knows where it might lead? Perhaps to the toppermost of the poppermost.

SECRET #163

Think irrationally. And often.

"I never made one of my discoveries through the process of rational thinking." - A. Einstein

What irrational thought do you have that others would dismiss out of hand? Might it help mankind in ways small or gargantuan? Do you have a method to keep things cold without destroying the planet? We could all use that.

Al Einstein was a guy who had a lot of ideas that took a while for others to accept. We all know the classic $E=mc^2$. But did you know he worked with fellow physicist Leo Szilard to develop a more energy efficient refrigerator?

At the time, traditional ice boxes were being replaced with modern machines that ran on electricity. Unfortunately (for the people able to afford them), they relied on poisonous gases like methyl chloride, ammonia, and sulfur dioxide as refrigerants. When newspapers reported the death of an entire family in Berlin due to toxic fumes from a broken refrigerator seal, Einstein and Szilard set out to find a better solution to prevent such a tragedy from happening again.

The need for irrational thinking helped them circumvent the standard wisdom of the day and use a heat source to provide coolant, with thermodynamics driving a combination of gases and liquids through three interconnected circuits.

Despite Einstein and Szilard's alternative designs for refrigerators, it was the introduction of freon in 1930 that propelled refrigerators from death traps to non-toxic storage units for cold cuts, ice cream, and leftover Chinese food. Today there is renewed interest in their design due to the impact of chlorofluorocarbons on the ozone layer. The need for alternative energy sources means humanity may yet benefit from the Einstein-Szilard Fridge.

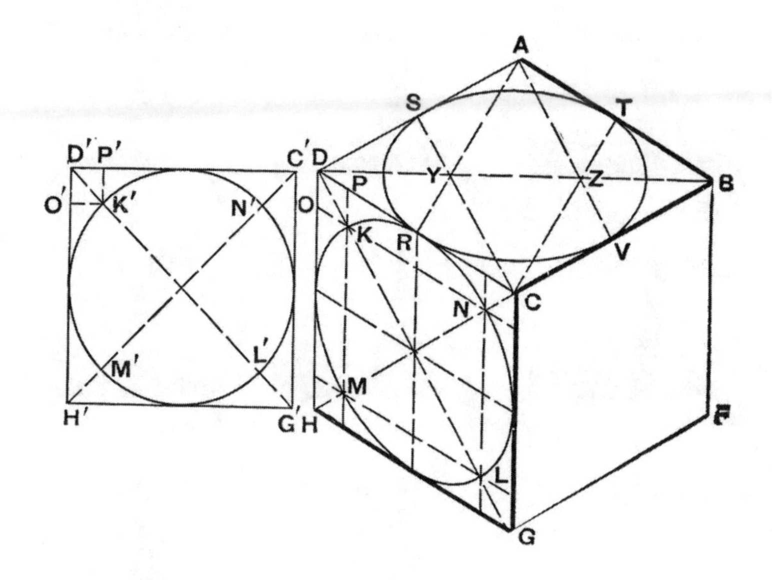

SECRET #185

TURN ON ALL THE FAUCETS.

A marketing executive once urged us to open every spigot when thinking about how to save a large account from exiting his firm. He meant for us to flood his office with ideas. It didn't work then…but it has many times since. Try it the next time you have a difficult problem to solve.

SECRET #129

Avoid the self-important.

The human being is the only animal that thinks building luxury condos, inflating their net worth, and being discussed on television makes them superior to one's fellow creatures. Yet a human is really only a slightly more evolved monkey with less body hair (most of the time). The more you remember this, the less likely you are to overreach your station, grab too many bananas, and eventually be imprisoned for tax fraud, bribing an FBI agent, or colluding with a foreign government. And if you're thinking of running for president, put a picture of a monkey on your campaign poster as a reminder not to get ahead of yourself. The other monkeys will thank you for it.

SECRET #154

Plan an elaborate funeral for yourself.

News conferences, state dinners, ribbon-cutting, photo ops...political leaders spend an inordinate amount of time stage-managing ceremonies intended to commemorate their successes. Small wonder, since they wouldn't have ventured into the business of pressing flesh and begging for votes if they weren't eager for attention. Yet their day-to-day activities pale in comparison to how much effort they put into planning their last rites.

Take John McCain. He spent a full eight months designing an elaborate ceremony to honor...John McCain. As the *New York Times* reported, "He obsessed over the music... choreographed the movement of his coffin from Arizona, his home state, to Washington. And...began reaching out to Republicans, Democrats, and even a Russian dissident with requests that they deliver eulogies and serve as pallbearers."

Now we don't want to cast aspersion on John McCain's motives for this four-day tribute to John McCain. He was a war hero and served the people of Arizona for much of his time on earth. And there is the thumb in the eye his ceremony was intended to administer to the sitting president. The question is: why should a grandiose spectacle be reserved only for those who spend their lives courting the limelight? Over-the-top memorials need not be the sole provenance of movie actors, senators, and members of the British monarchy. The unsung heroes of this country deserve special treatment as well. (Our definition of "hero" being anyone who puts up with various attention-seekers while going about the business of surviving this current age of unreason. Namely, all of us.)

We encourage you to begin planning your personal requiem now. Start putting aside a few bucks every week earmarked for "My Send-Off." Begin writing a set of instructions for your big day — or days — that specify exactly what you'd like to have occur. Fireworks, tap-dancing, power boat races: it's all fair game. Swap these instructions with your best friend. Whichever of you goes first, the other will circle the wagons (loaded with plenty of food and beverages, since you'll want to attract a crowd beyond mourners who actually know you).

Research the rules in your community for throwing a parade where your remains are the main attraction. The parade need not stretch for miles. It's perfectly acceptable to have your pals just walk your body up and down the street in front of your apartment. As for the coffin, why settle for the standard rectangular box? Better to be carried aloft in something that really represents your life. Have a custom wood-worker come up with something shaped like an airplane (if you're a pilot) or a fish (if you're an angler). Why not?

You may find that once you start planning this great event, you won't want to miss it by being deceased. So don't wait. Stage your funeral while you're still alive to enjoy it. "Playing dead" is way more fun than being dead. At least, that's what the ghosts in our life have told us.

An ice cream truck is a must. Make sure it's well-stocked with creamsicles and strawberry shortcakes.

SECRET #135

Shake your own hand.

There's an ancient proverb that states: "If your own house is not in order, how can you possible help another to tidy up theirs?"

So before offering a hearty handshake to a friend, colleague, or local law enforcement official, we suggest you give yourself one first. Clasp your hands together. Doing so is a great way to get centered and remember "I am here now." There's a reason your own two hands clasped together is the intercultural symbol of prayer and spiritual growth.

When you explore what your own hands feel like, you can learn things about your temperament and your personality. Are they hard and tense or soft and supple? Warm or cold? Damp or dry?* Grab a knuckle. Study your wonderful opposable thumb, the keystone of humanity's progress. Those hands are loaded with more nerve endings and wired with greater familiarity to your brain than any other part of your anatomy.

Artists since Da Vinci have believed hands are the most beautiful part of the body. Modern dancers know hands are the most expressive and subtle of limbs. And Tai Chi masters know that hands are the essential ninth gate for the transmission of energy. So slap your two mitts together, give them a good shake and say, "Hello, adorable friend." Sparking the divine in yourself is a great way to start the day.

SECRET #210

Always enter the office pool.

Many people put $2 in an office pool every time the lottery rises above a certain number...say $100 million. Then after many, many months of not winning, they start to question the practice. "Damn, I'm out $200 already with nothing to show for it. Maybe I should stop playing."*

There are two problems with that statement. First off, you do have something to show for it — brief periods of hope. For several hours, you get the opportunity to fantasize about your instant fortune and the dreams it will finance. Naturally, being the selfless giver you are, you'd give half of it away to deserving non-profits. Fortunately, that still leaves you richer than Croesus.

But the biggest reason to continue to play the office pool? Knowing what will happen the day you don't play the office pool. Your colleagues will win and you'll be watching everyone celebrate while staring into the abyss. $2 not to contemplate dying alone in an SRO while your former office mates are driving by in their Maserati Sport Convertibles? That's the greatest gift of all.

**Admittedly, you have a better chance of being eaten by a shark or knocked into the next world by a meteor impact than prevailing in the lottery. It takes a strong-minded person to ignore all that.*

SECRET #128

Look for the applause sign.

Performers expect to hear applause after they do their job. But why should this only be appropriate for actors, musicians, and public figures?

Getting applauded feels great, and everyone should experience this acknowledgement for their efforts. Hotel maids, traffic cops, baristas, coders, heavy equipment operators, massage therapists...all deserve a rousing cheer for a job well done. And while you're at it, give yourself a big hand for whatever you're doing right now. Successfully ordering a turkey sandwich? Three cheers! Navigating the bowels of Penn Station to make the 6:03? Hooray! Cleaning out your hall closet, the one you haven't touched in a decade? Huzzah! Remember, you deserve it.

Note: Researchers at Uppsala University in Sweden have discovered that applause is contagious, so the more you give yourself, the more others will join in.

SECRET #188

Take good care of your personal demons.

We don't need Halloween to remind us that human existence is one spooky ride.* Grotesque figures lead our public discourse and ghoulish creatures blare at us from media outlets large and small. Still, the celebration of witches and goblins does offer a reminder of a more intimate pursuit: the care and feeding of one's personal demon.

As opposed to the supernatural characters of mythology or Hollywood's evildoers, personal demons are our own concoctions, individually generated and having no independent existence outside our own bag of skin. One's demon can arrive at any moment. Though being demonic, they often decide to reveal themselves at the most inopportune times — particularly the wee hours when one is desperate for rest. So when your demon surfaces, what is the appropriate response?

It's helpful to understand that most demons simply want attention. Much like a faithful dog excited at the prospect of his master returning home, the demon has patiently waited for a quiet moment to say hello after being cooped up inside your subconscious all the day.

Say you wake up in a cold sweat and your demon is standing next to the bed, leering down at you. Some would advise you to attack your demon before he attacks you. That would only serve to hurt your demon's feelings. After all, he's made a perilous journey from the depths of Hades for this visit. "Battling your demon" is the equivalent of fighting yourself.

While counterintuitive, it's more advisable to embrace your demon. Here are a few suggestions for the next time he pays a visit:

1. Greet your demon warmly, like you would an old friend. Understand he is an extension of your personality; there's no reason to be frightened of yourself. Invite him into your domicile the way you would a relative. Take his cape and top hat and hang them nicely in the closet. Offer him the good chair and let him prop his feet on the coffee table, even if his boots are caked with mud.

2. Ask the demon what's on his mind. He'll probably be in a foul mood at first; usually demons arrive in a snit so let him rant for a while. You may find him lashing out at you regarding your personal failings or criticizing your latest mistakes at the job. Don't take it personally; be patient and remain detached. Eventually he'll let you get a word in edgewise. In the meantime, compliment him on his appearance despite his pale complexion. This should bring color to his cheeks.

3. Offer your demon something to munch on. Cake, pie, or ice cream are welcome choices; a little treat will help take his edge off. Extra whipped cream is advised if he's particularly snarky.

4. While he may ask for it, avoid giving the demon alcohol or narcotics. Demons tend not to react well when mixing chemicals with their volatile personalities. You want to soothe the demon, not trigger him.

5. Demons love to go for walks, especially at night. Where would he like to go? To the casino? An all-night bakery? Take your shadow self out for a stroll. Fresh air and exercise will do you both good.

6. Demons enjoy spirited conversation, not just internal dialogue. One way to get their full attention is to speak out loud to them. If you are out in public, this may appear as if you've lost your mind. Does this bother you? Simply strap on a Bluetooth headset and you'll look like you're in the midst of an "important phone call."

Ultimately, by showing the demon respect rather than anger, impatience or fear, you're helping yourself mend fences, soothe inner turmoil, and unify your bifurcated subconscious. Befriend your demon and he will befriend you.

**For Halloween this year, we suggest avoiding the top four costumes for adults (witch, vampire, zombie, pirate). Rather, dress as your own personal demon. It's more creative, and he'll credit you for the effort.*

SECRET #169

The everyday gravy boat.

None of us are promised another day, much less another government holiday, long weekend, or summer vacation. So why not celebrate the good fortune of being conscious and functioning at this very moment with deep and abiding gratitude. And gravy.

Thanksgiving comes and goes, and with it the blessed gravy boat. But why should this beacon of gastronomic goodness be relegated to brief appearances at holidays? Why not make gravy a staple of every meal? You have our permission to pull that gravy boat back out of deep storage, place it in the center of your dining table, and fill it to the brim with the following recipe. And if you're thinking we want you to soak up a high fat, high chemical concoction until your heart stops on a dime, take note: the following contains no gluten, grains, corn starch, flour, or filler of any kind. Pour generously at every meal. Breakfast included.*

INGREDIENTS:

- 1 quart organic low sodium chicken broth
- 2 large onions, roughly chopped
- 6-8 cloves peeled garlic
- ½ tsp dried thyme

- Salt and pepper to taste
- 1 tablespoon coconut aminos
- 2 tablespoons ghee, unsalted butter, or coconut oil

Start by dumping the broth, onions, garlic, and thyme into a medium saucepan and bring to a boil on high. Then switch the heat to low and let it simmer for thirty minutes or until the onions and garlic are really soft. At this point, taste for seasonings and add salt, pepper, and coconut aminos. Then pour everything into a blender, add two tablespoons of ghee, and blitz everything until it is uniform. Voila!

**But lay off the biscuits. Those things are like edible hand grenades for your body. Reach for some pineapple instead.*

PARABLE #7

Transatlantic failures? Or worldwide heroes?

In 1927, Charles Lindbergh received acclaim for piloting *The Spirit of St. Louis* across the ocean — the first non-stop solo transatlantic flight.

Yet two weeks before, French aviators Charles Nungesser and François Coli also attempted the journey in an effort to win the $25,000 Orteig Prize. Strapped into their biplane *L'Oiseau Blanc*, they took off from Paris for New York, only to disappear before arrival. The remains of their plywood and canvas-covered plane have never been officially recovered.

To this day, the disappearance of *L'Oiseau Blanc* is considered one of aviation's great mysteries. Creating a great mystery is an amazing accomplishment in anyone's book, and eighty years later their attempt continues to be the source of investigation and conjecture. How many pilots from yesteryear are celebrated with a rooftop restaurant in Paris named after their doomed biplane, featuring a delicious "pâté en croûte" complemented by artichoke and foie gras from Aveyron? Further proof that bad outcomes need not equate with failure and could lead to fine dining opportunities in the world's most romantic city.

As every SuperOptimist knows, it's in the attempt that life is best measured. All hail Nungresser and Coli, true heroes who tried their best.

SECRET #130

Appropriate times for breakfast.

As the most important meal of the day, any time is the right time for a game-changing, mood-altering breakfast. We offer this list of great breakfast times to get your mood back on track.

- 5 a.m. Breakfast ahead of the curve.
- 7 a.m. The classic early breakfast.
- 9 a.m. A civilized start.
- 10 a.m. The mid-morning booster.
- 12 noon. Breakfast makes for a great lunch.
- 2 p.m. Breakfast pick-me up.
- 4 p.m.The early dinner breakfast special.
- 6 p.m. Five-course breakfast.
- 8 p.m. The dessert breakfast.
- 10 p.m. European elegance by late breakfasting.
- Midnight. Breakfast with the night owls.
- 2 a.m. After-hours breakfast with rock stars and truckers.

Performance experts advise a basic formula for breakfast: Pair carbohydrates with proteins for best results.

SECRET #192

Go full swami.

A person interested in "mindfulness" today is often told to begin their practice by meditating for twenty minutes at a time. They're also encouraged to download a Headspace app, buy a special cushion and mat, purchase a statue of the Buddha, and sign up for a weekend retreat in the Catskills.

In India, it's a bit different. There a teacher would tell a beginner to start by meditating for six hours a day — no questions asked. Six hours of meditation a day may seem excessive. But if you want to gain the benefits of pure consciousness, twenty minutes won't cut it. In time, whatever practice you undertake can ultimately grow to twenty-four hours a day. It goes beyond sitting on a custom made zafu waiting for the chimes on your iPhone to go off.

So how do you go from zero to six hours all at once? Teachers point to the practice of "Japa" -- repeating a mantra or a divine name over and over again so it takes root in the mind. Whether you choose "om," "1-2-3-4," "Hare Krishna," or "cocoa butter," filling the mind with a simple word or sound will lead the practitioner away from the grasping, clinging and suffering generated by material world pursuits and move you towards a higher realm of existence. To expedite your practice, we recommend you join a like-minded sangha or spiritual group so you can gain energy from others on the same path.

Here's to detaching from the madness of the material world. This includes transcending trade wars, the cancel culture, and the quandary over wishing someone a "Merry Christmas" vs. a "Happy Holiday."

SECRET #159

Fun with deprogramming.

We may think we operate on the strength of our own free will, but the truth is, we're all members of cults to some degree: the cult of the smartphone, the cult of stationary bikes, the cult of artisan cheese boards.

Still questioning your cult status? Ask yourself, "Is that really me in those retouched Instagram photos or is it a reflection of belonging to yet another social media cult?" What can we do about our entrapment? While there are experts who can perform interventions to undo the brainwashing, here's a short guide to deprogramming yourself whenever you feel the need:

1. **Step out of the matrix.** Remember you exist in the middle of a vast scheme that has secretly created all your cravings and desires. By detaching for a moment, you can reassert your power of authority over your inner Pavlov dog.

2. **Turn from cult to creativity.** The best way to get even with group-think is to make some art that has nothing to do with success, beautification, or professional sports teams.

3. **Seek knowledge from experience, not the Internet.** All too often, we turn to the latest reports, studies, or YouTube videos to find out how to handle our prob-

lems. This is another form of cult-like behavior. Instinctively, you know how to handle what you're facing better than a whole day googling "Why do I have body dysmorphia when looking at pictures of Olga Sherer?"

4. **Read a good book.** Here are some suggestions, but don't take our word for it. Go to the library and see what your hand touches first. 1) *My Year of Rest and Relaxation* – Ottessa Moshfegh 2) *Instant Zen* – Thomas Cleary 3) *Winnie-the-Pooh* – A.A. Milne.

There are lots more ways to deprogram yourself and reboot your internal mainframe. At least these can get you started when you find yourself sinking in the quicksand of societal conditioning. Here's to freeing yourself, the sooner the better.

Even the last of the self-sustaining hunter-gatherers, the Bushmen, now face government pressure to "get with modern life." Despite English lessons and alcohol availability, they prefer their freedom.

SECRET #182

Every day is Opening Day.

Normally associated with the beginning of the major league baseball season, we see no reason why Opening Day should only be relegated to balls and strikes. Here are some suggestions for celebrating that go beyond a nearby stadium or tavern.

Open a window. Indoor air pollution has been described by the EPA as a primary environmental health problem. In addition, the American College of Allergists states that 50% of all illnesses are caused by polluted indoor air. So fling wide the windows. You'll be glad you did.

Open a jar of sauerkraut. In addition to going great on a hot dog (the classic opening day meal of baseball enthusiasts), sauerkraut has amazing health benefits that help offset the harmful qualities of the frankfurter.

Open your third eye. Known as the 'Ajna chakra', the third eye is a source of intuitive wisdom and has the potential to lead you to the highest form of intelligence. Try meditation with eyes closed, focused on the area between your two actual eyes. Once you start seeing a bluish-white light, you're halfway to healing your chakras and getting in touch with a further dimension of existence.

Open your browser and search for "Smead Jolley." There's nothing more enjoyable than discovering arcane knowledge about some of the more colorful players of yesteryear. Jolley was an outfielder in the 1930s who once committed three errors on a single play.* But did Smead let his ineptitude in the field get him down? No. After getting dumped from the majors due to his poor fielding skills, he spent the rest of his career hitting the cover off the ball in the Pacific Coast League. Oh, and his nickname was "Smudge." You can't ask for more from a ballplayer.

**First, he let a ball roll through his legs in the outfield. After allowing it to carom off the wall, the ball rolled back between his legs in the opposite direction. When he finally recovered the ball, he heaved it over the third baseman's head and into the stands. The ump took pity on him and only scored it two errors.*

It's this kind of attitude that will serve you well in life.

Double that if you own a diner or a pharmacy.

SECRET #179

Let the weeds take over.

We owe the start of lawn maintenance to the British aristocracy of the 1860s. These sophisticates first introduced the idea of the "weed-free lawn" in an attempt to show affluence. Before this trend took over, people actually pulled grass out of their lawns to make room for the weeds, which were often incorporated into family salads and herbal teas.

Today, homeowners proudly display their "green thumb" by making sure their yard is chemically micromanaged like a Martha Stewart dinner party. Most have no idea that this carpet of toxins ranks just above bare concrete as a pox on our planet. To which we say: let thy lawn go native! Not only will this positively impact the environment, you'll have more time for the simple pleasures of fresh air, blue skies, and hammock naps. Plus you'll gain an appreciation for the beauty of wildflowers and learn to love such growths as “Digitaria Sanguinalis."

If you still have a hankering for landscaping, it's best to choose species indigenous to your area, rather than planting exotic trees and shrubs with no concern for their geographic origin. The local variety produces more insects, which in turn attracts birds that provide a check on pests. It is personalized conservation at its best, or what landscapers refer to as “biophilic design” -- integrating nature into our modern environments. Even better, knock down your house and live in the wild. Your neighbors might object; it can take a while for humans to accept change. Offer them some tomatoes and beans from your new organic garden and perhaps they'll think twice about calling the town's Planning and Zoning Commission to have you removed.

While you're at it, let what you see in the mirror take its natural course. You'll save a fortune on razor blades and hair gel.

SECRET #193

Your fascination quotient.

Since humanity started with primates known as the Ardipithecus, miracles have become so plentiful in life that we take them for granted. Yet reframe your perspective and suddenly the things you ignore become jaw-dropping revelations. Here are a few examples that we find deserving of deeper appreciation:

DAILY COMMUTE: We take a "train" pulled by a "diesel engine" that runs on "steel tracks" from one "state" to another. That's amazing!

PLACE OF EMPLOYMENT: We work in a "52-story building" that has twenty-one "elevators" and 189 "water fountains." That's amazing!

LUNCHTIME: We eat a "pulled pork sandwich" from a "food truck" and they give us an "extra side of coleslaw" to go with it. That's amazing!

FORTUNE: Twice a week we buy a "ticket" that qualifies us to win hundreds of millions of "dollars" if our numbers are chosen. That's amazing!

We could keep going and you can too. First close your eyes and click your heels together. Then remember that you have eyes to close and heels to click. Amazing, isn't it? Now open your eyes, point at the nearest object, and marvel at it out loud.

"Wow, that's a 'metal file cabinet' that contains sheets of 'paper' with 'words' and 'pictures' on them. That's amazing!"

Note: You may need to explain to onlookers why you are behaving like this, as they probably aren't as attuned to the miracles of everyday existence as you are.

SECRET #225

When in doubt, think scientifically.

Consider the memories which you consciously or unconsciously pull up on your personal "hard drive." If those memories are negative ones, you relive the feelings of the situation and can get stuck in the cycle of repetition. If they're positive ones, you might go chasing after whatever it was that turned you on in the first place. Neither reaction is recommended.

Treat your brain as you would any other piece of technology. By understanding your thoughts are merely electrical impulses which rise and fade, you can teach yourself to switch off the information that's not serving you well. This way, thoughts lose their power to control you. A repetitive mantra can also help to short-circuit the noise. Eventually your reactions to these mental images will dissipate and you won't be held captive any longer. Some call this "freedom." But not insurance agents, politicians, and marketing executives. They would prefer you act upon every impulse. Thinking scientifically, you can ignore them too.

SECRET #166

Get rich while enjoying nature.

It's only human to want to amass a fortune, and the quicker the better. Anyone that says they'd prefer to barely make ends meet is what Italians call "un bugiardo."

Investing in the stock market is one way to attempt the speedy accumulation of wealth. Yet timing the market only works for government officials, corporate insiders and that neighbor who smugly claims they got out "just before the crash," even though they're still driving a 2003 Impala. Your money is better spent at the racetrack, where at least you have the satisfaction of tearing up your ticket while enjoying the beauty of horses in full gallop.

Which brings us to an activity that's affordable, offers you exercise and plenty of fresh air, and gives you the opportunity to add to your net worth: the search for buried treasure. Finding old coins, jewelry, and relics from past generations is a heck of lot healthier than sitting around staring at a stock ticker. Why, a 1936 Buffalo nickel is worth more than 100 times its value today and is sure to keep going skyward. All you need is a sense of adventure and the visual acuity to spot the precious items in your path.

Of course, you'll have a lot more success if you deploy your own metal detector. We recommend a lightweight model that's easy on the back, with enough features to make your search a fortunate one. Having done the research, we prefer the Garrett AT Pro. It has 40 different settings to help you uncover various types of ferrous metals. And it's fully submersible up to ten feet.

Venturing outdoors with your metal detector is a reward in itself, leading to aerobic fitness, healthier heart, improved circulation and flexibility, and increased vitamin D levels. Even if you find nothing, you've found nature — and that's the richest experience of all.

Remember to consult with a numismatic expert before polishing your treasures too vigorously. The value of the old coins you uncover can be destroyed with too much scrubbing and scratching.

SECRET #187

Daydreaming? Don't let us disturb you.

We may think daydreaming is a voluntary part of our cognitive motoring, but it actually accounts for up to half of all our waking thoughts. Of course, some people view daydreaming as a form of procrastination. The suits in corporate are apt to chastise an employee with their feet up, pencil slack, and a thousand-mile stare on their face. But don't let the nabobs of negativism get you down. "Deliberate daydreaming" is both good fun and 112% necessary to generate ideas that can propel the world forward.

To experiment, try shifting your focus away from whatever is in front of you (computer monitor, packed subway train, half-eaten fruit salad) to the "default mode network" of the brain, which can spark better ways of problem-solving. Pre-loading an area of interest before takeoff can focus one's dreaming, making for time spent more wisely.

It's high time to celebrate the brain activity that occurs when eyes are open yet focus on the external world is relaxed. What else in life can offer pleasurable escape from the confines of reality, yet not cost a dime or leave a scar (assuming you don't identify as a somnambulist)?

Note: If it becomes difficult to emerge from the spaced-out state once you enter it, it could be a condition known as "Maladaptive Daydreaming." If so, seek professional counseling.

SECRET #186

Take yourself on a spacewalk.

Landing on the moon was the height of accomplishment for the Apollo 11 astronauts. But government-sanctioned space pilots are not the only ones with the ability to launch themselves into orbit. With a bit of concentration, you can too.

All you need is SuperOptimist Antigravity Reconnaissance (SOAR), a method of picturing the world from above. It can be as simple as imagining yourself gazing down from the ceiling at an event transpiring in the room in which you're sitting. Or as far-flung as having your gaze come from another galaxy, rendering the world as a mere blip in the cosmos.

With a little practice in mental teleportation, you'll gain a perspective that renders any situation manageable. By looking at present circumstance as if standing on your own private observation deck — one that you can shift to any elevation — suddenly the traffic jam you're in becomes a curious abstraction, the endless office meeting a gathering of bobblehead dolls, the blank piece of paper a simple square of white without the power to paralyze. In fact, just by leaning back in your chair when you're working on something difficult, you can ease the strain and improve your ability to cogitate.

Whether stuck in a cubicle, or an airport, or an endless

holiday gathering, it's quite useful to teleport upward. With Antigravity Reconnaissance, you'll enjoy a way of seeing that puts everything — yes, everything — into perspective.

Should you wish to take this further and become a NASA-sanctioned astronaut, the following is required:

1. *Be a U.S. citizen.*
2. *Possess a master's degree in a STEM field, including engineering, biological science, physical science, computer science or mathematics, from an accredited institution.*
3. *Have at least two years of related professional experience obtained after degree completion or at least 1,000 hours pilot-in-command time on jet aircraft.*
4. *Be able to pass the NASA long-duration flight astronaut physical.*

SECRET #152

Bosk in your own magnificence.

The bosk, or common bush, resembles the human in many ways. It is messy and multi-layered; thick in some areas, patchy in others.

But that's where the similarity ends. While people are apt to complain about the slightest problem, the bosk remains imperturbable in its approach to life. It lives in concert with its surroundings. It asks nothing of others. It requires no heavy care or maintenance. The bosk is neither envious of its flowering neighbors, nor takes pity on those considered less fortunate. The bosk does not wish to trade its unkempt appearance for that of the manicured hedge, row of daffodils or climbing ivy. The bosk is comfortable in its own skin, no matter how many layers of itchy vines and bushy leaves hide its Jackson Pollock-like skeleton.

The bosk watches bemusedly as bi-peds march past, busy with their efforts to landscape every square inch of yard. People like to try controlling nature, but the bosk knows it's a fool's errand. Take a lesson from a nearby bosk and relax into your surroundings. It will do you a world of good.

SECRET #203

Your next vacation starts now.

While you can't light out for the Hamptons whenever the CEO does, you can always take a holiday anytime you like. We term this an "Immediate Vacation" (I.V.) — a momentary respite from gerbil-wheel cogitation that goes a long way towards renewing your energy, your mood, and your sense of humor.

So what constitutes a proper I.V.? Start yours now with the following steps:

1. Place pictures of your last vacation on your desktop. This will spark memory association of pleasant times while also lowering your blood pressure.

2. Keep a tube of sunscreen in your drawer and take a deep sniff when tension builds. This will both ignite the senses and return you to a time of peaceful clarity.

3. Go for a short stroll. Researchers at Columbia University found that exposure to sunlight, radiation, moving air, and water generate feelings of alertness, mental clarity, and elevated mood. So your Immediate Vacation may be as simple as leaving the office and walking around the block.

4. Close your eyes, place both feet on the floor,

> and breathe deeply through your nose for thirty repetitions. If anyone asks what you're doing, continue with another thirty reps. If they threaten to call security, take your lunchbreak early.

The Immediate Vacation is at the ready whenever you need. And unlike exorbitant hotel and airline charges, it's 100% free.

DID YOU KNOW? The Adirondacks inspired the first use of the word "vacation," as in: "One vacates from the city to exchange humid heat for fresh air." In a similar fashion, one may vacate from work to exchange stale thinking for fresh ideas.

SECRET #167

Curry for breakfast? Why not?

In America, we've been socialized to believe that a "hearty breakfast" consists of flapjacks, sausage, cereal, juice, and the like. Could there be a more exciting way to break the fast than what's on the menu at your local coffee shop?

One suggestion is adding some inner heat to your morning meal. It's certain to wake you up, since hot spices release endorphins in your system, similar to a runner's high. A nice breakfast curry with roti and a poached egg is a perfect start to the day.

But it's not just Asian countries that like their mornings spicy. In Pakistan, it's Siri Paya in the a.m., a soup made from slowly cooking the head and feet of a cow, a lamb, or a goat, then adding tomatoes, onions, and spices.

Mexicans like huitlacoche with their eggs. Technically speaking, this is diseased corn, sporting a fungus that's considered a delicacy in Mexico. The spores that infect the corn turn it black and give it a mushroom-like flavor.

And in Pennsylvania Dutch country (near where the first SuperOptimists were born), leftover scraps from the pig like the eyeballs, tail, and snout are ground into a patty with spices and fried, much to the horror of those thinking sausage is the worst thing that can be done with a sow's innards.

ALSO RECOMMENDED: Secret #169

SECRET #121

You're in luck.

We could all use more luck in our lives. So how do you persuade fortune to shine its flashlight on you going forward? British psychology professor Richard Wiseman examined the difference between self-professed lucky and unlucky people. He found that the charmed ones are those open to new experiences. They're more willing to talk to new people and try different things.

Of course, it never hurts to carry a special charm, or talisman, to improve your luck while you're going about meeting new people and doing different things. This object may not actually hold any special powers or magical conductivity, but the important thing is that you believe it gives you an edge. With that belief comes better juju. (You know, juju, like in *Silver Linings Playbook*.) We're partial to evil eye keychains, a counterintuitive way to keep Dame Fortune on your side. The evil eye is a curse believed to be cast by a jealous glare or other negative energy which is usually directed towards a person who is unaware. By carrying one, you'll be protected from dark spirits and bad luck. It also can't hurt to keep some Chinese Emperor coins in your car, kitchen, backpack, and valise. Round with a square-shaped hole in the center, they are said to be a representation of earth surrounded by heaven.

Now if all this isn't enough for you, why not go full Wiccan and cast some good luck spells for prosperity, love, and health? We advise reading up on this before you start your "abracadabras." Errant invocations can have unwanted side effects. You don't want to turn anyone into a frog by mistake. Although if you do, please take it to a local nature preserve so it can live in peace.

Carrying a pair of lucky dice can't hurt either.

SECRET #138

Better than sex. Better than drugs. Better than sex and drugs together.

If you can only muster one mind-body activity today, make it a genuine gut-busting, milk-out-the-nose-spraying, rip-snorting, teeth-baring laugh. You don't need a doctor to tell you that laughter instantly relieves your body's stress response, burns calories, and gives a positive jolt to your immune system, but it is funny that social scientists have spent millions of dollars to research this point.

In the right hands, even hideous, ungodly trauma can be funny. (Or not. This all depends on how elastic your sense of humor is.) Take Robert Schimmel, a professional funny-man whose eleven-year-old son died of leukemia. While he was devasted as a dad, as a comedian, his job was to find something to balance the gloom. This is what he came up with: "My son's last request when Make-A-Wish came was to see his father get oral sex from Dolly Parton. To this day, his wish remains unfulfilled."*

**At the end of his career, Bob Schimmel needed a liver transplant, was being sued for divorce from his much younger wife and had moved back in with his parents — at which point he was killed in a car accident. Schimmel mined each of these experiences to make people laugh. Except for the car accident.*

SECRET #184

Hug a nurse today.

Here at headquarters, we don't spend a lot of time looking at calendars or clocks. So imagine our surprise when we discovered that National Nurses Week had already come and gone. Fortunately, we remembered another tenet of SuperOptimist practice: celebrate whatever you want, whenever you want.

We hereby extend the observance for nurses indefinitely and encourage you to recognize the healers in your life. Not just the hospital variety, who will be working overtime due to the human need to drive too fast, forget to apply SPF 50, or peel a carrot without focusing on knife skills, but the mother who fusses over every sniffle and scrape, the neighbor who rushes over with a roll of gauze after you slip with the electric hedge trimmer, the son or daughter who administers to the visiting parent as if they were about to expire, or the concerned friend who hasn't heard from you in twenty-four hours and calls repeatedly to make sure you're still among the living.

As for a gift? We recommend getting a large tattoo of your favorite nurse on a forearm to show your unwavering devotion. Remember: nurses work hard and always provide care and comfort, even if it's the result of a mistimed water ski jump. They deserve more than a thank-you card. May the celebration continue!

SECRET #131

Be ready for your Elvis moment.

In August 1953, an obscure country boy named Presley walked into the offices of Sun Records. He aimed to pay for a few minutes of studio time to record a two-sided acetate disc: "My Happiness" and "That's When Your Heartaches Begin."

He later claimed that he was merely interested in what he "sounded like," although there was a much cheaper, amateur record-making service at a nearby general store. Biographer Peter Guralnick thinks that he chose Sun in the hopes of being discovered. Asked by receptionist Marion Keisker what kind of singer he was, Elvis responded, "I sing all kinds." When she pressed him on who he sounded like, he repeatedly answered, "I don't sound like nobody."

Elvis couldn't imagine what was coming next for him. The future is hidden until it happens. If you knew what was in store for you, life wouldn't be nearly so interesting. So maybe it's time for you to head down to Memphis. Who knows what might come of it?

Once you have your moment, you may be able to give Cadillacs to all your friends, just like the King.

SECRET #173

It's Sensory Deprivation Time.

Not long ago in human history, it was easy to find peace and quiet just by wandering outside at night and gazing up at the stars. But most of us now live in urban areas, not in the Atacama Desert in Chile (where astronomers do their best work unencumbered by light pollution).

In this era of sensory overload, it's a nice respite to unplug from the artificial. Since it's impossible to remove the outside stimulus completely, we advise taking away one of your own senses for a few hours and see how this modifies your way of thinking. A blindfold is a good start. Without the use of your eyes, what do you conjure? Researchers from the University of Rochester have found that even in absolute darkness, we still think we see. The question is, what images are visible to you when you're in the dark? Is your hearing more acute? How about your sense of touch or smell? Pick something up from your desk and roll it around in your hand. Interesting the difference between a roll of scotch tape and a cup of coffee, no?

If you wanted to try this experiment without a mask, there are still a few places on Earth that you can go. Among them are The Dark Sky Reserve on Ireland's Iveragh Peninsula or the NamibRand IDSR in Africa. And if you want your neighborhood to go darker, why not join the International

Dark Sky Association, which keeps track of light pollution and monitors how much darkness you really get in places across the globe.

SECRET #172

Let pink do its part.

If you've ever felt like the walls are closing in, maybe it's not the walls — it's the color. Hues and shades can play a big role in your mood. Take your cue from prison wardens who paint their holding cells pink. They were inspired by studies conducted by research scientist Alexander Schauss, who created "Baker-Miller Pink" and showed it to reduce inmates' hostile behavior. (The color is also referred to as "Drunk Tank Pink.")

Model Kendall Jenner painted her living room Baker-Miller Pink and raved about how it made her feel calmer while acting as a diet aid. "Baker-Miller Pink is the only color scientifically proven to calm you AND suppress your appetite. I was like, 'I NEED this color in my house!' I then found someone to paint the room and now I'm loving it!"* Kendell's use of ALL CAPS shows she may want to consider painting the entirety of her house this way.

Of course, one person's pink might be another person's chartreuse. So we advise you to experiment to find the color that puts you in the desired state. Blue, for instance. Blue does such a good job in calming the mind that after blue lights were installed at Japanese transit stations, there was an 84% decrease in the number of people jumping in front of trains. And last we checked, there were 260 shades of blue in the color spectrum to choose from.

SECRET #164

Extra tolerance in the age of zero tolerance.

A Muslim, a Catholic, an African American, a Jewish person, a Hispanic, a WASP, a Native American, a lesbian, an old woman, a gender-neutral individual, a Chinese communist, a Russian oligarch, an Iranian mullah, a red state Republican and an Upper West Side Democrat walk into a bar …

Have you smiled? Or are you getting your back up at the possibility that someone could be made fun of as this story unfolds? This is a litmus test to your future well-being. Can you survive in the current cancel culture — without cancelling yourself out?

Let's start with the facts. Humans are the nuttiest creatures on the planet. Our ability to be "triggered" has become so sensitized that each of us now needs a personal injury lawyer just to leave home in the morning. Our "big brain/ thin skin" combo leaves lots of time to parse language, self-select into special interest groups, and worry over slights both real and perceived. Each person would prefer it if other people agreed with their opinions. Each person would also like the freedom to render judgment on those who don't.

Tribal hostility has been going on since homo sapiens first noticed differences in their appearance ("Hey, you're not wearing the same bearskin as me. I'll feel safer if I make fun of your outfit!") and will no doubt continue despite corporate offices hanging up "Zero Tolerance" banners. Humans love conflict, and deep down they love feeling superior to other humans, even when that superiority is based on how "caring" or "woke" they are.

SuperOptimists understand that an individual's differences should be respected and celebrated. We also know that being overly sensitive is not an enjoyable way to go through life, as you become predictable, boring, whiny and people refuse to hang around you (except for other overly sensitive types). We're all fallible creatures, after all. Making fun of ourselves is a tonic for all colors of skin, sexual preferences, religious convictions, or gender reclassifications. Chortling at our failings is one of the core emotional expressions of joy. Who has ever wanted to turn away more spiritual joy — besides ruthless dictators and Ebenezer Scrooge?

So if you think you're special because you're a "woke white," go fuck yourself! And if you think you're special because you're multi-ethnic, or a member of a fringe group, or call yourself "they" instead of "he" or "she," go fuck yourself! As for us, writing this post with the superior attitude of know-it-alls, we'll go fuck ourselves too! See? Now we've all got something in common!

As for the joke that started this column, the fact that there is no ending is what's funny about it. To us, anyway.

SECRET #194

Inertia vs. risk: which side are you on?

Conformity is so normalized, we are barely aware of it. Each day we bow to safe, established standards. One could compare the act to a river that wants to remain within its banks, since altering its course may cause unanticipated upsets, flooding, and chaos.

But maybe a little chaos is exactly what one needs to renew the spirit. We invite you to join us in deviating from your norm and trying something outside your comfort zone. Of course, if you decide to tell your friends about your actions, prepare for the pushback you'll receive. "You're going to do *what*?!" "Don't you need to get permission for that?" "If you were going to ___________, don't you think you would have done it before now?"

Take their admonishments in stride. They are startled by your awakening. Let their incredulousness be your motivation. Know that there is immense social pressure to conform and stay in one's habitual role. Japan demonstrates this particular problem in the popular saying "出る釘は打たれる."

Admittedly, if nobody showed up for thankless tasks, social order would fall apart in a matter of days. But don't worry; most people are content to continue with their narrowly-defined jobs, activities, and labels, while you go in search of the new.

SECRET #199

Your fear removal kit.

Unless you are an anthropoid or alien, sometime in the last twenty-four hours you had a moment of doubt, worry or alarm.

It might have been fear of losing your job. Or possibly you distrusted a friend or partner's feelings for you. Maybe you worried that fire or storms would destroy your home. Or had a nagging feeling that eating a chocolate eclair might actually kill you. You might even have a fear of Halloween. (This is termed "Samhainophobia" and originates from the ancient Celtic festival of Samhain, when people would light bonfires and wear costumes to usher in the darker time of year — and ward off ghosts.)

Whatever your trepidation, how do you get rid of gnawing anxiety, creepy shivers, or full-blown panic?

Start by thinking of one scary thing that's on your mind right now. Whatever your boogeyman is, say the word out loud. Be it "sharks" or "elevators" or "corporate administrators." Giving voice to your fear can make you realize that what spooks you is mostly living in a dark corner of your mind and is not an imminent threat. If sharks scare you and you live in Kansas, the worry is not a real threat. If you work on Wall Street and have a fear of farm threshers, you're good for now.

Now take it a step further: think about the worst thing that could happen if your fear actually materialized. What if that shark found its way to Kansas and bit your leg clean off? It's true your professional tap-dancing career could be over, but you might still go on to win a gold medal in the Paralympics. If you lost your business, lost your faithful dog, lost your spouse or lost your mind, it could be the start of a bold new chapter in your life adventure.

The point is, when your worst fears happen, it is never game over. You will always have the power to change your attitude, even in difficult situations. What about death, you ask? The silver lining to that cloud is finally getting a good night's sleep. May you vanquish your fears once and for all!

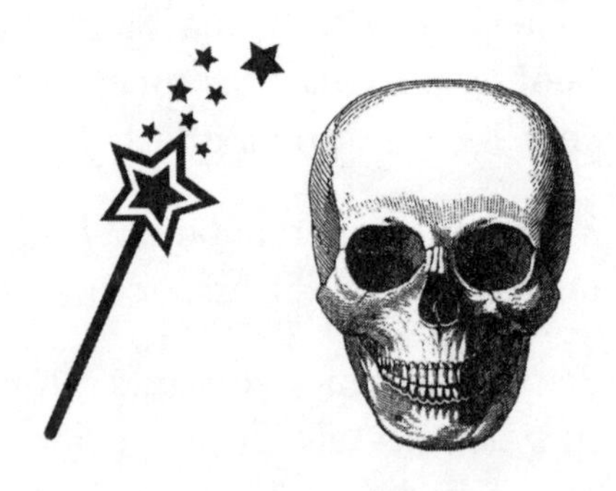

SECRET #212

Dead spouse? What an opportunity.

Edgar Allan Poe, master American author and proto-goth innovator of the macabre, knew how to make the best of things.

In 1835, Poe, then twenty-six, obtained a license to wed his thirteen-year-old cousin, Virginia Clemm. They were married for eleven years, by all accounts a loving and respectful match, filled with true romance. One evening in January 1842, Virginia showed the first signs of consumption (now known as tuberculosis) when she indelicately vomited blood while playing the piano. Virginia lived another five years in a state of pallor and lingering sickness as she approached the grave. But Poe turned this horrific situation to a creative bent, developing a theory that "the death of a beautiful woman" was the "most poetical topic in the world." His masterpieces of gothic writing, like his most famous poem, "The Raven," explore themes of death, sickness, and the ghostly lives of captivating young women who happen to be deceased.

There are opportunities in the worst situations for a true SuperOptimist. As Edgar said, "To die laughing must be the most glorious of all glorious deaths!"

SECRET #189

Forgetting more than usual? You may be a genius.

Recently, a friend expressed concern that their memory was heading south. "I just finished this great book about New York last week. It's called... uh... oh, my god, what's the name of it... this is frightening... I can't remember anything anymore!"

None of us are immune to the effects of aging, especially regarding memory. We forget stuff all the time (and are constantly being reminded of it by our well-meaning family members). But rather than freak out when we call Dave "Don", or think Millard Fillmore was the 14th president of the United States,* we give ourselves credit for forgetting. Why? Because it's a sure sign that we are highly intelligent.

Scientists at the University of Toronto suggest that the struggle to find the right word, whiff on a name, and blank on a fact are all signs you're super smart. They posit that forgetfulness is important, as it's merely the brain making space to take in more crucial information, the kind that helps you make better decisions going forward. Will knowing that Jason Bateman starred as the Mutant in *Mr. Magorium's Wonder Emporium* help you survive another day on Planet Earth? Probably not. So forget it.

The next time you have a memory lapse, don't think you're "losing it." Instead, know that you're simply taking the time to empty out your overloaded brain tank. To help, we've created this list of the things really worth remembering:

1. Date of birth.
2. Credit card number/expiration date/four-digit code.
3. Name of spouse or significant other.
4. Which local pizza establishment serves the best garlic knots.
5. Cleanup hitter for your hometown baseball team.
6. Company you work for and your immediate superior.

**Fillmore was actually the 13th president. Speaking of chief executives, do you know the names of all forty-nine? (Hint: that's a trick question.)*

SECRET #211

The beauty of going backwards.

Humans have long taken pride in their ability to "push forward" and "tackle the challenge ahead." Yet even if you're dead set on getting somewhere in life, there's much to be gained from spending part of your day moving in the opposite direction. Here are some simple activities that underscore the benefits of going in reverse, both mentally and physically.

Walk backward: Native American folklore suggests that 100 steps backward are as good as 1,000 steps forward. According to present-day health experts, that's not just a spiritual maxim. Incorporating ten minutes of backward walking or jogging a few times a week provides you with increased body coordination, improved sleep cycles, stronger leg muscles, sharpened thinking skills, and better balance. Who couldn't use more of those?

Heal backward: Modern medicine continues to turn back the clock in favor of treating the whole person and not just the outward symptoms of disease. Even general practitioners have begun prescribing the same tinctures and plants the Chinese were using 2,000 years ago. Fasting, reiki, micro-dosing mushrooms? The hippies were ahead of their time.

Record backward: Backmasking is a recording technique in which a sound or message is recorded backward onto a track that is meant to be played forward. Backmasking was popularized by The Beatles, who used backward instrumentation on their 1966 album *Revolver,* particularly the guitar solo on "Tomorrow Never Knows." (Note: the later chant of "Paul is dead" when playing "Revolution Number 9" backwards was a concoction of an overzealous fan in Michigan and not an example of backmasking.)

Think backward: Da Vinci often wrote backwards, his notes only decipherable when held up to a mirror. Ginger Rogers is praised for having done everything Fred Astaire did — but backwards. Philip K. Dick wrote an interesting novel about people experiencing life in reverse, starting with death.

Age backward: Is this really possible? Scientists are working on it.

Talk backward: It's interesting to note that the ability to recite the alphabet backwards is used both as an indicator of giftedness in children, and as a measure of sobriety in adults.

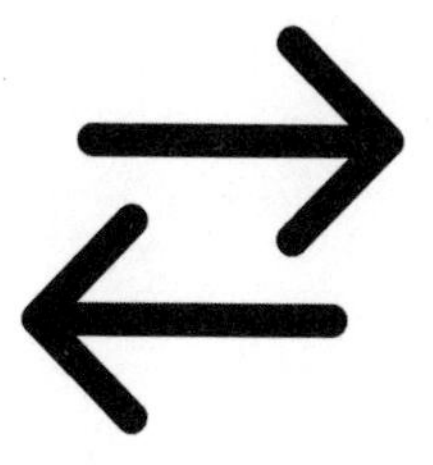

A reminder that January 31st is "National Backward Day." Using reverse logic, you could celebrate it now.

SECRET #140

A volume at random.

a. Travel to your local library.

b. Closing your eyes, walk down an aisle.

c. Pull a volume chosen at random from the stacks.

d. Without looking at the book, turn to a random page.

e. Now open your eyes and read the first paragraph at the top right.

f. Whatever is in that paragraph, allow it to inspire an action corresponding to its contents.

SECRET #204

The gods are ready to assist you.

Are you amenable to letting spirits, extraterrestrials, and mythical beings into your space? Are you prepared for energy shifts? For images, color, and light to enter your consciousness? For dissociation from what people consider "reality?"

The practice of channeling — a person's body being taken over by a spirit for the purpose of communication — has been around for millennia. Channeling involves shifting your mind and mental space in order to achieve an expanded state of consciousness. There are countless stories of shamans, witch doctors, prophets and others who summon higher beings or receive supernatural knowledge from the spirit world.

Think of it as plugging into a vast cosmic switchboard or tuning a radio to get a clear signal. As you enter the spirit realm, you become receptive to higher frequencies. Let the universe decide to deliver the message and you be the monitor so others can receive it.

Channeling is often stronger when you're active, be it exercising, dancing, creating, walking in nature, meditating — the times when you're focusing with your heart and not your logical mind.

So go ahead and do whatever comes naturally, from a bit of toe-tapping to automatic drawing to full blown mania.* It also helps if you maintain the innocence of a four-year-old when summoning your god. They are much more likely to show up if you do.

**Some might question your behavior when summoning your gods and goddesses. Ignore them. They will soon learn that you have entered a higher realm of being and wish to follow you there.*

SECRET #207

It's never too late to rebrand yourself.

At one time, the top-ranked university in the United States was known as the "College of New Jersey." That certainly doesn't sound as impressive as "Princeton," does it?

The Nobel Peace Prize was born from a desperate attempt by Alfred Nobel to reframe his story as something other than the inventor of dynamite.

And did you know that Pabst Blue Ribbon, beer for drinkers on a budget, has convinced the Chinese to pony up $44 a can for its "Blue Ribbon 1844" version?

The point is, there's nothing the world likes better than a good story, and you definitely have one to tell. If you need to exaggerate a bit? All the better! That just proves you have a healthy imagination and a disregard for the rules — those pesky details imposed by people to keep the majority of us in line.

Think of where you want to go, decide what story it will take to get there, and then rebrand yourself to fit your goal. If it takes coming up with a new name for yourself, remember you're in good company. Right, Amelia Kelly?*

**Today known as "Iggy Azalea".*

SECRET #156

Upon realizing life is not everything you hoped for.

Our suggestion? Turn to the "Holy Moly Doughnut Shop." Or the "Spooky Scary Skeletons." Or "The Smeeze."

We're speaking, of course, about getting your groove on. Sure, dancing might not be the first thing that comes to mind when having a Sartre moment. But just because you're no longer in high school doesn't mean you shouldn't dust off your best moves and take every opportunity to go full out to the music.

To start, think of the positive effects on your body. According to Dr. Nick Smeeton from the University of Brighton, when you're doing "The Whoa" or "The Swagg Bouncee," you expend more than 300 calories every half-hour, equal to a run or swim. All of that starting, stopping and changing directions burns a ton of fuel even though you're not covering a lot of ground. The up-and-down and side-to-side movements of dance may likewise activate and train many of your body's little support muscles and tendons.

The psychological benefits are also impressive. Some shrinks have prescribed dancing as an effective therapy for those who suffer from social anxiety or fear of public speaking. The idea: if you can loosen up enough to do "The

Renegade" in front of strangers, you're a lot less likely to feel self-conscious when hanging out or speaking in front of an audience. Posting a video of yourself attempting to follow Charli D'Amelio's moves is a good way to ease into the practice.

It doesn't matter what you dance to — the latest Dua Lipa song or something a little more retro. Get those helicopter hands working and we'll see you...hopefully sooner than later.

Note: Any type of dancing contributes to SuperOptimism. Except for ballet. It's hard to be upbeat when standing "en pointe."

TRIAL BALLOON #1

The answer to America's problems.

Democrat, Republican, Libertarian, Green...whatever the party affiliation, Americans can't get enough football. We sacrifice things like better schools and public libraries to build massive stadiums to honor our local teams, and the high price of NFL game attendance — tickets average hundreds of dollars — doesn't stop all classes of people from rubbing shoulders as they fill these fishbowls to near capacity each Sunday (except during pandemics).

So how can we marry the much-adored game of football with the unwieldy, uncooperative workings of Washington? Let's form football teams along party lines from the three branches of government. The winner of a game of football between the Elephants and the Donkeys could decide if a bill winds up in the trash can or enshrined as a law. It could determine if the Supreme Court hears an argument against Arctic Drilling or leaves it in the lower courts. Even allowing for a few hours for the losing side to complain about the refereeing, the fate of any important issue could be decided in just a day or two.

If laws were decided through football, the American people would be more engaged in civic duties than ever. For one thing, it would make the process of governing fun to follow. As much as we talk, text, and tweet our opinions about politics, the day-to-day activities of each branch are extremely dull and nearly unwatchable. It feels like divine intervention when CSPAN leaves a poorly-attended House debate to cover a Presidential motorcade, but that's not saying much. Now consider the audience for a show that combines sports talk with political commentary. A ratings bonanza!

Governance through football — may it lead us forward as one nation, indivisible, with liberty and slant patterns for all.

PARABLE #8

Thus spake King Larry.

We've never looked at television host Larry King as an oracle, at least not until his death. Only then were we made aware of a quote attributed to him that could be the simplest explanation of how to navigate the vicissitudes of life.

“If you have passion, a chip on the shoulder, a sense of humor, and you can explain what you do very well, it doesn't matter if you're a plumber or a singer or a politician. If you have those four things, you are interesting."

Perhaps Larry was only referring to whether you'd be a decent subject for one of his interview programs. But he could well be stating what all the monks, priests, scholars, and philosophers have spent centuries and volumes trying to define as a "life worth living." Let's break it down:

1. Like Ishmael, what is your great white whale? Do you have a strong and barely controllable emotion about something in your life? Whether it be the arts or fiduciary accounting, pursue it until your EKG reads "zero".* Even if there is little chance of success, the Sisyphean climb up your mountain will produce plenty of strong memories and interesting fodder for psychiatrists, sociologists and yes, talk show hosts to study.

2. Believe in yourself. No matter how uncertain, insolvent, or unbalanced you are, put that chip on your shoulder and don't let anyone knock it off. Who are they to question your love of ice baths?

3. Giggle long and hard, and at your own screwups most of all. For those who can chortle at the absurdity of the world tend to live until at least eighty-seven years of age.*

4. Get a story and stick with it. Even if you have many interests, many side hustles, and many dreams, formulate a simple narrative about yourself and repeat as often as necessary. (In King's case, that started with his name.)

**Utilizing his own four-point system detailed above, Larry managed to beat the actuarial table by a good eight years.*

SECRET #170

Returning to square one? How fortunate.

Whether it's a stalled career, the end of a relationship, or recurring doubt concerning one's spiritual practice, people consider starting over to be a real bummer of an experience. Going back to the beginning is considered the mark of failure in a world that celebrates winning, victory, and happy endings.

But we're here to tell you that square one is a super place to be. For that square is your square. And your square, by definition, is perfect, with each side equal to the other three sides.

Scientists are always having to confront their failure to prove a theory and start afresh. Mahayana masters talk about starting over with every breath, to be in the moment with each exhalation and inhalation. And let's not forget all the wonderful artists who have spent a career working with, around, and into squares. Joseph Albers and Mark Rothko come to mind. So before cursing the gods for hitting a dead end, frustrated at having to reinvent the wheel yet again, remember that starting from scratch is something to celebrate.

Also remember that the origin of the phrase "square one" originates from radio broadcasts of European football games. To help the listener visualize the action, the field was divided into a grid of imaginary squares, with square one centering on the goalmouth. Interesting that square one is actually closest to the goal.

Welcome back.

PARABLE #4

The fewer people at your sendoff, the better.

Who was the true author of American independence? Many say Thomas Paine was the guy. A radical writer who emigrated from England to America in 1774, his pamphlet *Common Sense* was read by every colonist questioning their fealty to Great Britain. No less a figure than John Adams was quoted as saying: "Without the pen of the author of *Common Sense*, the sword of Washington would have been raised in vain."

Yet despite playing the greatest role in moving the American people from a spirit of rebellion to one of revolution, he was later ostracized due to his ridicule of institutionalized religion. Thanks to his seminal work *The Age of Reason*, only six people attended his funeral in 1806. It's tough being a truly independent thinker. But don't let that stop you. Who needs a big crowd noshing on your tab anyhow?

PARABLE #9

The fortune cookie is always right.

No matter what you've done in the past,
your future is spotless.

SECRET #160

Inspect all snowstorms.

Many centuries ago, Zen monks of the Rinzai school disavowed the notion of man's superiority to animals, plants, water, fire, or even the earth itself. These monks spent years communing with nature, never seeing another person as they retreated to the mountainous caves to meditate. They reached out their hands to the universe and became one with it. Their practice equipped them with the skills to handle both the isolation and the elements in good health.

Later, 19th Century naturalist Henry Thoreau wrote of his fondness for solitude, wandering alone through the forests, beaches and back roads of Massachusetts. In fact, he gave himself a position which demanded he strike out from his one-room cabin no matter what the weather. "For many years I was self-appointed inspector of snowstorms and rainstorms, and did my duty faithfully ..."

Should you face weather deemed "inclement," consider what Henry would do. He'd bundle up, head outside, and lose himself in the day. Not content to simply traipse through the cold, he would pause to listen to a storm and its special characteristics. He'd look closely at the snowflake, marveling at the amazing symmetry of each hexagonal formation. He might measure the accumulation or sketch the scene in his notebook.

When you see the wind start to howl or the flakes start to fall, why not go inspect them yourself? And while you're at it, don't forget to cozy up to a tree and offer it a gentle pat on the trunk. Give a plant a warm greeting. Say hello to a small pile of dirt, or a nice fat rock, or a bird that has seen fit to stay close rather than flying south. All of a sudden, you have an infinite number of new friends* who remain constantly by your side, in "good" weather and "bad."

**But take care with the snakes, you never know if they are poisonous.*

SECRET #ZZZ

This calls for a nap.

In addition to a hearty mug of hot cocoa, we find there's nothing like a short rest to reinvigorate the senses. (Unless, of course, it's a long rest. Both rate high in our book.) Now the nation's military leaders agree. According to the recently issued "Army Field Manual," the armed forces have officially embraced an afternoon snooze for sleep-deprived soldiers.

"When regular nighttime sleep is not possible due to mission requirements, soldiers can use short, infrequent naps to restore wakefulness and promote performance," the manual states. A stage two power nap, encompassing fifteen to twenty minutes of snooze time, is recommended to reset the system and produce a burst of alertness and increased motor performance. The slow-wave nap lasting thirty to sixty minutes is good for decision-making skills, such as memorizing vocabulary or recalling directions. Going for sixty to ninety minutes of napping, complete with REM activity, plays a role in solving creative problems.

Let's not forget the hypnagogic, or micro-nap. The Greek philosopher Aristotle believed that true inspiration could be found in the state of half-wake/half-sleep when the brain slips into an impressionistic state. Albert Einstein, Thomas Edison and Salvador Dali would take micro-naps in order to stay in Stage 1 of sleep so they might tap into vivid imagery and sensation.

In Dali's case, his naps lasted less than one second at a time. How is this possible? He held a key or spoon between his fingers so when he nodded off, the clang of dropped metal would awaken him. Dali claimed that "slumber with a key" revivified both mind and body, as well as generating powerful visual ideas. Of course, being Salvador Dali probably helped.

SECRET #126

Take the George Washington cure.

Whether you've got a cold, or virus, or melancholia, or something that's not yet in the medical textbooks, be comforted by the fact that many have been in worse shape — and even survived to become president.

Before George Washington concerned himself with the health of our nation, America's first commander-in-chief had to contend with an amazing array of personal afflictions. During the course of his life, he dealt with smallpox, malaria (six times), diphtheria, anthrax, dysentery, tuberculosis (twice), quinsy, carbuncle, and pneumonia, to say nothing of losing all his teeth. It's only fitting that there's a hospital in D.C. named after him.

While George needed some luck to make it through these gauntlets (not to mention a brutal war with the British), it's important to recognize the capacity of the human organism to fight sickness. Of course, one should take care of the body along the way. To this end, George exercised faithfully, supped and grogged in moderation, tried to get the proper sleep, and avoided tobacco.

He also believed in balms and nostrums to keep the grim reaper at bay. According to records from his presidential library, among the items he ordered from an English apothecary in 1759 were the following:

- 6 Bottles Turlingtons Balsam
- 8 Oz. Spirit of Lavender
- 1/2 lb. Ipecacuane powderd
- 1/2 lb. Jallop powderd
- 12 Oz. Venice Treacle
- 4 Oz. best Rhubarb
- 12 Oz. Diascordium
- 4 lb. Pearle Barley
- 4 Oz. Balsam Capevi
- 5 Oz. Liquod Laudanum
- 5 Oz. Spirits Hartshorn
- 4 Oz. Spanish Flies
- 3 lb. Bird Lyme
- 6 lb. Oyl Turpentine
- 2 lb. Linseed Oyl—cold drawn

- 4 lb. Allam
- 1 lb. Spirma Citi
- 4 Oz. Tincture of Myrrh
- 4 Oz. Balsum Sulpher
- 4 Oz. Pulvus Basilic
- 2 Oz. Mer. Dulcis
- 4 Oz. Salvolatile
- 10 lb. Hartshorne Shaving
- 2 Quarts strong Cinamon Water

While many of these treatments are no longer popular, rhubarb has plenty of antioxidants and lavender is used for insomnia, acne and hair loss. But please take it easy with the laudanum. It contains a mixture of opium, alcohol, morphine, and codeine. It's doubtful a doctor would prescribe this today, but you can ask.

George ultimately died of epiglottitis at age sixty-seven, a ripe old age for the early 1800s.

SECRET #205

Create your own snow days.

Snow days are one of the great spontaneous joys of life. There should be more of them, and they shouldn't just be relegated to bleak days of winter. With the right attitude, you can experience a snow day any day of the year.

One way to get started is by placing a snow globe on the nightstand. When you wake up, give that snow globe a good shake and watch the flakes dance merrily in the glycerin contained within. Now decide whether this day should be a "regular day" or a "snow day." If it's the latter, go back to sleep for as long as you like. (Naturally, it helps if your snow day falls on a "summer Friday" or you are self-employed, but this shouldn't be a deal-breaker. A veteran snow-day conjurer can always create an excuse that passes muster with the powers that be.)

Granted, it's a bit harder to conjure a snow day when the heat index creeps up to 105. But with a box of cocoa mix and some comfortable pajamas, there's no reason why you can't declare a snow day right now if you want to.

See Secret #160.

PARABLE #6

No bad way. No good way.

And now, we pause to let Jianzhi Sengcan, the Third Patriarch of Zen, remind us that no situation need trouble us. Here are the first stanzas of Sengcan's "Hsin Hsin Ming,"* containing all the instructions required for avoiding suffering and removing every obstacle to enlightenment. (And all in just eighty-six words.)

The Great Way is not difficult
for those who have no preferences.
When love and hate are both absent
everything becomes clear and undisguised.
Make the smallest distinction, however,
and heaven and earth are set infinitely apart.

If you wish to see the truth
then hold no opinions for or against anything.
To set up what you like against what you dislike
is the disease of the mind.
When the deep meaning of things is not understood,
the mind's essential peace is disturbed to no avail.

To remind ourselves to practice at every opportunity, we've boiled "the Ming" down to its two key components: “No preferences. No problems.” (At four words, it’s even harder to forget.)

And in case you're wondering what "Hsin Hsin Ming" actually means, different translators have rendered the title in different ways. Here are a few to ponder:

1. *On Believing in Mind (Daisetsu Teitarõ Suzuki)*
2. *On Faith in Mind (Dusan Pajin)*
3. *Trusting In Mind (Hae Kwang)*
4. *Trust in the Heart (Thomas Cleary)*
5. *The Perfect Way (translator unknown)*

SECRET #178

Toss the earbuds.

Lots of people like to clamp on headphones and drown out the noise around them. But why be tethered to electronics when there are fascinating sounds being created around you twenty-four hours a day?

Take the average commuter train. Each moment in transit provides a veritable symphony. Close your eyes and listen to the low hum of the ventilator system mixing with the staccato crunch and squeak of the train car navigating the tracks. Add the wrinkle of a newspaper and the crackle of the electrical wires, along with an occasional blast of the motorman's horn. The basso profundo of the conductor coming over the loudspeaker harmonizes with the business executive spraying directives into her mobile phone. At times, the mixture rivals that of the most accomplished modern composer.

Exit to the street and the music changes. Keeping your eyes closed is more difficult while navigating the sidewalk, so we recommend finding an empty bench in which to continue your listening tour. Of course, you may be startled by a loud backfire from a truck, or someone bellowing that there's a big sale at Footlocker. Work them into your composition.

With your newfound appreciation of the sounds that others take for granted, perhaps you will follow John Cage and write a concerto inspired by your experiences.

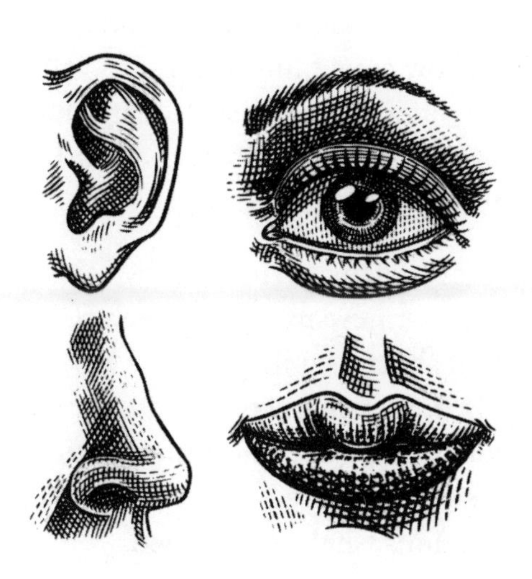

SECRET #139

Cut yourself loose.

Emerging from the ashes of World War One, Dadaists saw society's view of "normalcy" as irrational and created art that completely challenged traditional views of class, religion, politics, technology, and morals. Their reactions to society's hollow constraints are just as valid today as they were a century ago, when Tristan Tzara published a short poem on how to free yourself from rigid thought with an act of anti-authoritarian aplomb.

Découpé (or *cut-up)* is performed by taking any piece of linear writing — a newspaper article, a page from a book, the instruction sheet for plugging in a Wi-Fi router — and remodeling it in a spontaneous and uncontrolled way. By doing so, you will bypass the inner critic who demands that things be neat, ordered, and understandable. Here are Tzara's instructions, slightly modified.

1. Take some scissors.
2. Cut out each of the words that makes up the piece of writing.
3. Put the words in a bag, a hat, or shoebox.
4. Shake gently.
5. Remove one word at a time from the bag.

6. Copy the words in the order in which they left the bag.

7. The poem that you construct will resemble you.

While a newspaper article is perfectly good material for your initial foray, we prefer taking an expensive book that society has deemed important and cutting up a page, proving that even "great art" should not be considered untouchable. This is a good step to freeing yourself completely from the social construct and letting the super-ego know who's boss.

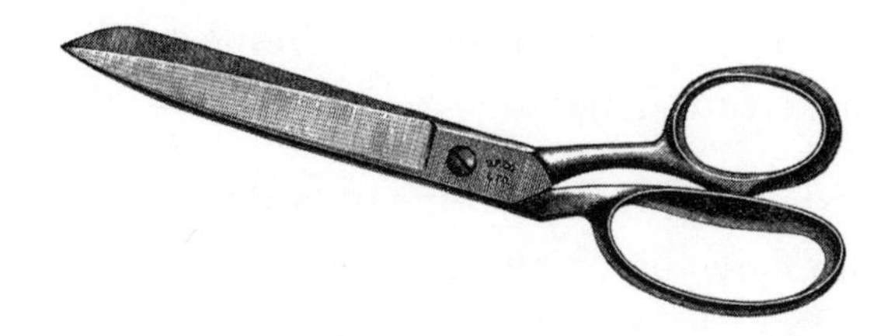

TRIAL BALLOON #2

Let's make April 1st a national holiday.

That which seems the height of absurdity in one generation often becomes the height of wisdom in another.

– Adlai E. Stevenson

When someone calls you a fool, do you take offense? Or thank them for their perspicacity?

The wise among us realize that our foolish nature is something to be embraced — and as often as possible. The godmother of show business reinvention, Cher, says, "Unless you're ready to look foolish, you'll never have the possibility of being great." Like other renegades, Cher advocates freeing the wild child inside you rather than timidly hiding beneath a veneer of "respectability" if you want to make your mark.

So the question is, how will you embrace foolishness today? What pranks are you planning to shake up the status quo? What could you do tomorrow, next week, or next month that will have the office, local pub, or family den buzzing with conversation after the shock wears off? And is one day really enough to play the fool card, or should we advocate for more time to really explore this vitally important side of life?

At the very least, the United States could follow the example set by the city of Odessa in Ukraine. Here, the first of April is a holiday, complete with a festival that includes a large parade, free concerts, street fairs, and performances. Festival participants dress up in a variety of costumes and walk around the city playing pranks with passersby.*

One could argue that businesses giving their employees the day off to act foolishly could wind up generating the brainstorms that lead to a better planet for all. And quite possibly, a major boost in productivity. Try it and see what happens.

In 18th Century Scotland, they did Odessa one better, as the April Fools tradition was a two-day celebration starting with "hunting the gowk" in which people were sent on phony errands, followed by "Tailie Day," which involved pinning fake tails or "kick me" signs on people's backsides. Not that we want to give you any ideas.

SECRET #128

Give yourself a low-maintenance makeover.

They say, "When you look good, you feel good." So what change can you make to improve how you feel?

According to scientists from Harvard and Boston University, applying bright color to the lips not only makes the wearer feel more confident, others will also perceive you to be more reliable and competent. Researchers also discovered that students who wear makeup actually score better on tests. Wearing cosmetics apparently leads to overall enhancement in self-esteem, attitude, and personality that carries over to the exam room.

While these studies were conducted on women, we're confident that in this age of experimentation and fluid gender roles, men can also benefit from a bold choice of color.* After all, guys weren't shy about applying foundation a few hundred years ago. An 18th century gentleman usually owned a dressing-box that held his razor cases, scissors, combs, curling irons, oil and scent bottles, rouge, and powder. Even soldiers wore wigs during this period.

A hundred or so years later, androgenous rock stars of the 1970's (and 80's and 90's) weren't shy about accentuating their attitude with makeup. The New York Dolls made red lipstick the cornerstone of their first album cover.

So if you want to give your day a boost, score better on multiple choice tests, or provoke discussion on that next zoom call, you may just find dabbing on some Tom Ford Scarlet Rouge provides the spark you're looking for.**

**The market for men's cosmetics is predicted to grow $49 billion this decade.*

***Of course, if you prefer using your natural gifts to win friends and attract people, remember the words of Dale Carnegie: "A smile costs nothing, but creates much. It enriches those who receive, without impoverishing those who give."*

SECRET #176

Seek information outside the usual sources.

As an intelligent person who wants to arrive at their own conclusions — or better yet, be surprised by a discovery that 2 billion people haven't already seen via memes on Facebook — you need a way to navigate the network that bypasses the biases, especially your own. One favorite is the Wikipedia "Random Article" button. Just today we clicked and discovered the following fact we had no clue about:

Moneva is a municipality located in the province of Zaragoza, Aragon, Spain. According to the most recent census, the municipality has a population of 123 inhabitants.

Now what will we do with such information? Maybe nothing. Maybe we'll move there. But one thing's for certain: Staying open-minded is the surest way to gin up enthusiasm for each new day ahead. As Philip Stanhope, the 4th Earl of Chesterfield, stated: "Let it be your maxim through life, to know all you can know yourself; and never to trust implicitly the information of others."

The official flag of Moneva.

SECRET #165

5 thoughts to age better by.

Philosophers, savants, and sages have said that with age comes the wisdom of experience. Here are a few nuggets we've amassed over the course of 122 years on earth (collectively speaking):

1. The best way to approach life is as a series of experiments, while maintaining a sense of humor about the results.

2. If you do something and it feels risky and likely to fail, it is also filled with potential for learning something important.

3. Be yourself. Most people get this one wrong.

4. As you get older, you become free to have crazier ideas. And because you are closer to death, less is at risk.

5. You can win at any game with lucky timing.

SECRET #177

Show your ghosts the door.

According to novelist Henry Miller, "Once you give up the ghost, everything follows with dead certainty, even in the midst of chaos." If you're tired of trying to do something because you aren't getting what you want from your efforts, try giving up that particular ghost today and see if that doesn't bring more sunshine into your life. If not, invite a fresh ghost to take up residence inside your person. At least you'll be haunted by the specter of something new.

SECRET #145

Be the Betty you can be.

Want to extend your lifespan by 15%? Research shows that the odds of living to age eighty-five and beyond is aided by the type of thinking you do.

"I know it sounds corny, but I try to see the funny side and the upside, not the downside," Betty White said in a recent interview. That's right, Betty knows it's best to look at every situation, even the crappy ones like her first marriage to a rural chicken farmer that lasted six months, and at least get a laugh or two out of it. You'll also find vodka, hot dogs and red licorice on Betty's training table. As Betty is proving, it's not just optimism, it's *SuperOptimism* that can propel you to the century mark in style.

SECRET #168

Enjoy your greatest success after death.

At the beginning of 1903, Gauguin was living on an island in Polynesia and engaged in a campaign designed to expose the incompetence of the island's gendarmes, in particular Jean-Paul Claverie, for taking the side of the natives in a case involving the alleged drunkenness of a group of them. Claverie, however, escaped censure. At the beginning of February, Gauguin wrote to the governor, François Picquenot, alleging corruption by one of Claverie's subordinates. Picquenot investigated the allegations but could not substantiate them. Claverie responded by filing a charge of libel against Gauguin, who was subsequently fined 500 francs and sentenced to three months' imprisonment. Gauguin immediately filed an appeal in Papeete and set about raising the funds to travel to plead before the judge. At this time he was nearly penniless, very weak and in great physical pain. He resorted to using morphine and died suddenly on the morning of May 8, 1903.

Nobody thought too much of his passing, but one hundred and ten years later, Gauguin's painting *Nafea Faa Ipoipo* (*When Will You Marry?*) sold for $295,000,000 to the museums of Qatar, becoming one of the most expensive art objects ever. The artist achieved his greatest success long after departing this mortal coil. Who knows what you'll be worth once you've departed?

ADDENDA

YOUR QUARTERLY HOROSCOPE

Mercury in retrograde? That's great news.

Meetings cancelled, elevators stuck, phones malfunctioning, promises broken, limbs broken, blood clots revealed — it seems everyone we know feels the effects whenever Mercury goes retrograde. In fact, just trying to type this paragraph, our laptop screen froze and we had to hit "restart."

But there's a positive aspect to the zodiac zeitgeist that people fail to take into consideration: Mercury retrograde is a great excuse to not do anything you don't want to. SuperOptimists look for this kind of rationale all the time.

Using the "Gosh, I wish I could. If only it wasn't Mercury retrograde." excuse, you can turn down the cocktail party invitation from that colleague who bores you to tears. You can claim "computer trouble" for continuing to miss the deadlines the boss gave you. While you're at it, you can postpone those pesky chores around the house and cancel your plan to wade into weekend traffic to visit the relatives. Knowing it could all go haywire, it's better to leave well enough alone.

Remember, 90% of people on the planet know their astrological signs and 70% read their horoscopes regularly, so the majority will understand when you beg off due to planetary misalignment. Meanwhile, if something weird actually happens to you during this period, look at it as a positive: this planetary event is drawing attention to some part of your life that you've been ignoring. Rather than avoid the issue, embrace the turbulence and see if you don't come out better for it on the other side.

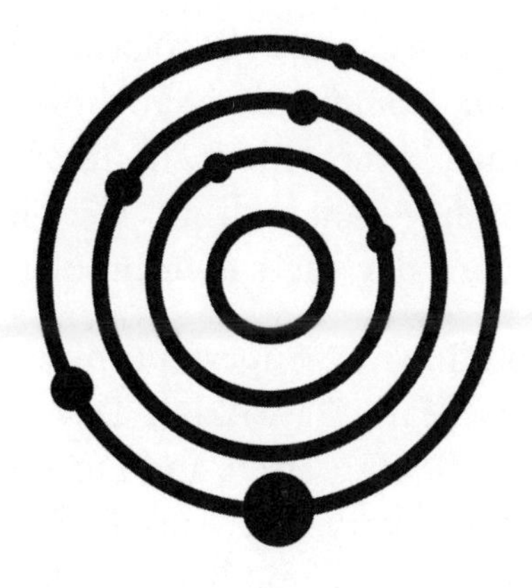

Mercury is 48 million miles away and often obscured by sunlight, so no one really sees this apparent retrograde motion occur — even astrologers employing a three-inch Newtonian reflector telescope with 300 mm focal length lens.

ANNUAL PERFORMANCE REVIEW

Quit vaping. Stop dating losers. Learn how to code. We are constantly under self-imposed pressure to halt our bad habits, right all our wrongs, straighten our posture, update our resume, and lose fifteen pounds.

But what's wrong with eating a chocolate bar while watching reruns of *Buffy the Vampire Slayer* anyhow? Ignore the life coaches with their exhortations to improve everything about yourself. If they want to drink celery juice and get on the scale five times a day, that's their problem, not yours.

Here's the resolution the SuperOptimist always adopts, whether it's New Year's Day, Arbor Day, or just another Tuesday: "All is well, life is swell, and I'm good just the way I am." By accepting every screw-up, flaw, and mistake as the price of being human, you have a 130% better chance of enjoying life fully.

Resolution defined is "the firm decision to do or not do something." Why not make a firm decision to not make any decisions about your future, and enjoy all 365 days without putting undo pressure on yourself? You might find this turns out to be "your year" after all.

Another good exercise is looking back on what's worked previously. Here's a short quiz to separate your pluses from your minuses. By doubling down on the good stuff, you'll be assured of more personal victories in the coming months.

MY ANNUAL PERFORMANCE REVIEW

1. What was the best thing I've experienced so far?
2. What was a huge waste of my energy?
3. What activity gave me the most pleasure?
4. What was my bravest failure?
5. What can I try that I haven't already tried?
6. What error can I avoid now that I see it?
7. What did I fear that I survived?
8. Did I handle the bad shit well?
9. How many times did I feel joy?
10. Who did I like hanging out with?
11. Who would I prefer never seeing again?

VOCABULARY CHALLENGE #1

Four simple words that will change your life for the better.

One SuperOptimist practice we never tire of? Adding the phrase "And isn't that great!" to any thought we may be having. A recent example is illustrated by the following:

"Oh, my, I've just broken a molar on a macadamia nut. Now I'll have to see a dentist. And isn't that great!"

By adding these four magic words, you've taken a rather pedestrian situation in which pain, expense, and inconvenience are the assumed outcomes, and reframed it into something that may have positive consequences. After all, who knows what might happen at the dentist? You could meet a new lover in the waiting room. Your dentist might have received a fresh tank of nitrous oxide and offer you some. You could decide to go for an additional ultra-whitening session and walk out of there looking like Hollywood royalty. Your dentist might accidentally find you have a serious lesion in your mouth that was going to kill you if you hadn't seen him in time.

Here's another one:

"This winter chill is brutal. I'm freezing my tuchus off. And isn't that great!"

Why is it great? It's great because the cold helps you burn body fat, leading to a slimmer figure. It's great because the cold keeps away invasive insects, like the Asian Tiger Mosquito. Most of all, you can take comfort in the fact that you can go indoors and make a cup of hot cocoa to ward off the chill.

One more: "With my mediocre attempts at painting, I'm never going to be the next Van Gogh. And isn't that great!"

Why is that great? The pressure on you to be the next artistic success has been lifted, freeing you up to do more experimental work that may one day be celebrated. And while we can't be sure, your psychotic episodes probably won't lead you to severing your own appendage, unlike the struggling post-impressionist.

VOCABULARY CHALLENGE #2

Three magic words that will set you free.

For some reason, humans have a very hard time admitting that they may not have all the answers. It's hardwired in our DNA to never admit we're clueless or wrong. And yet the strength, the wisdom, and the relief in saying "I don't know" may be the smartest thing a person can ever communicate — no matter what their age, sex, race, or position in society.

Is it any surprise that our most effective leaders are those flexible enough to change their opinions based on the latest intelligence, rather than fearing the appearance of indecisiveness? It takes a big person to say, "I don't know." And how refreshing it is to hear.

As author and rabble-rouser Ken Kesey said, "Once you have the answer, you stop thinking." And who wants to do that?

VOCABULARY CHALLENGE #3

Eight words to spark adventure.

There's nothing like making a list to whet the appetite for derring-do. Here are some words that may help spark your own escapade.

1. blindfold
2. wager
3. zingily
4. slingshot
5. gotch
6. luftmensch
7. precipice
8. zhuzhy

**Bonus words: prop plane, Monaco, splashdown.*

APPENDICES

APPENDIX #1

The SuperOptimist Personality Indicator

Who am I?

What career should I be pursuing?

Where do I fit in?

SPI is the only self-administered test you need to get on the path you belong. This science-based method of self-evaluation and assessment will help you discover where you stand now, and where you should head next. Use the information to move forward with confidence.

START YOUR TEST NOW.

1. Thinking about technology, I experience the following feeling:

   a. Terrified that robots will soon take my job.

   b. Excited about receiving Universal Basic Income.

2. I believe Pavlov's dog was:

   a. Placed into indentured servitude against his will.

   b. Lucky to have achieved a measure of fame compared to other dogs.

3. When I turn on my computer each morning:
    a. I feel like the day will be filled with endless drudgery.
    b. I review my Instagram, Facebook, twitter and Pinterest feeds and by then its lunchtime.

4. When taking public transportation, I am preoccupied with thoughts of:
    a. How late I will be to my next appointment.
    b. The thrill of casino gambling.

5. Given the choice, I'd rather:
    a. Accept the world for what it is.
    b. Pay for a better experience.

Answer key: All are correct choices. Congratulations for exercising your decision-making skills.

APPENDIX #2

Group Meeting Guidelines

While gathering in collectives to practice SuperOptimism is not required, it has proven beneficial for some. Here are the meeting guidelines established by the first such encounter group in case you're thinking of starting one in your area:

1. Shoes and shirts not required.
2. Meetings begin with one minute of vigorous yodeling.
3. No chairs. Standing keeps energy levels up, promotes good posture.
4. Free coffee and doughnuts at minimum. Steak Frites if evening session. Those with disposable income buy for everyone else.
5. Burning effigies fine so long as fire codes are observed.
6. Standard Quaker Meeting House procedures for sharing thoughts rather than "hand raising and choosing" exercise.
7. Basket passed for contributions. Then repassed for anyone needing money to take as "no interest loan."
8. Meeting ends with bending and stretching, then shouts of "See you in Santa Fe!"
9. Any deviation from this list not only welcomed but encouraged.

APPENDIX #3

Note to artists: Don't give up!

Being an artist is hard work, even if much of your time is spent staring at a blank canvas (or page, or screen). You never know when inspiration will strike — it could be today, it could be four years from today, it could be never. But one thing's for certain: if you were hunched over a desk working for The Corporation and you felt a big wave of creative juice coming on, you wouldn't be able to grab a brush and start painting, or sculpting, or whatever it is that you do. Hang in there. Try to avoid judging yourself for not being successful in the ordinary sense of the word. Meanwhile, get out of the house at least once a day and interact with another human being — preferably a fellow artist who needs the company.

Place your worst work here. Later you may recognize it as worthy of the encasement.

APPENDIX #4

Eat this book.

When Menelik II, former emperor of Ethiopia, felt unwell, he would eat a few pages of the Bible. Should you find yourself in Menelik's shoes, we suggest taking a page of SuperOptimist wisdom and consuming it with a liberal application of Frank's Hot Sauce.

A spot of tea is also recommended.

APPENDIX #5

Surprise page.

Surprises are great for the circulatory system. They get the blood moving and open the sweat glands. Every book should have a surprise inside, not just mysteries. Here's yours! (Assuming you weren't expecting a unicorn.)

ACKNOWLEDGMENTS

Thankfully, none of us are self-made. We are the product of many strange twists and turns, quirks and chromosomes, and the energies of creatures we meet along the way. We'd like to express gratitude to our families, friends, and canines who have supported us in this particular endeavor.

And in memory of Big Ben, Lady Jane, Dr. Bill Jr. and Anne.

PASS IT ON

In the spirit of giving, pass this book on to someone you believe could benefit from the suggestions contained within. Better yet, offer it to a complete stranger and exchange phone numbers. You might enjoy a spirited conversation later.

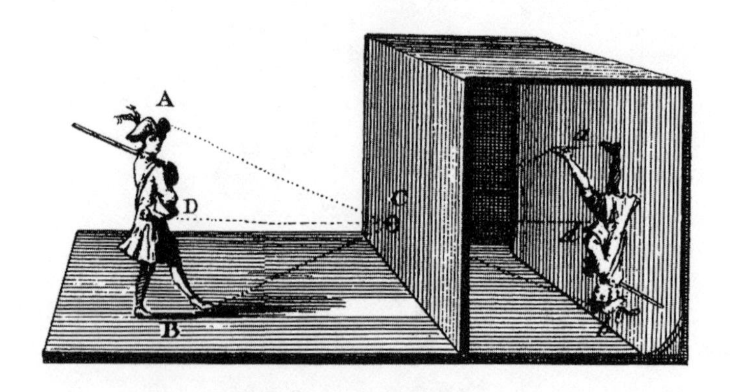
A
D
C
B

ABOUT THE TRANSMITTERS

Nathaniel Whitten and Walter Morton have been seekers of higher truth and optimal sensation for more than five decades. Since their encounter with the SuperOptimist, they've made it their mission to pass along this vital information to all who wish to receive it. Individually and collectively, they have studied shamanistic meta-psychology, Zen, wabi-sabi, neuro-muscular sciences, healing arts, traditional kung fu, tai chi, literary deconstruction, and the practical frugality that is indigenous to Pennsylvania.

They can be contacted for one-on-one consultations or corporate wellness seminars at The Institute for SuperOptimism headquarters, reachable via superoptimist@gmail.com.

DON'T BE A STRANGER

For the latest SuperOptimist thought transmissions, visit our digital headquarters at www.superoptimist.com.

SuperOptimist!

Yes.

Yes.

Yes.

Yes.

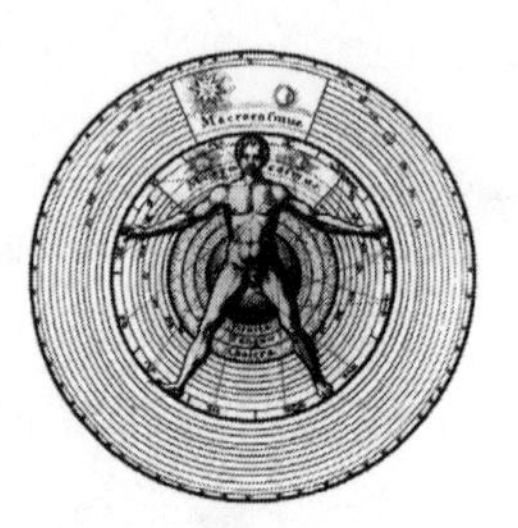

Yes.

Come back soon.